EASY COLLEGE COOKBOOK
For Guys

EASY COLLEGE COOKBOOK

For Guys

EFFORTLESS RECIPES TO LEARN
THE BASICS OF COOKING

Noah Daniel Stern

ROCKRIDGE
PRESS

For general information on our other products and services or to obtain technical support, please contact our Customer Care Department within the United States at (866) 744-2665, or outside the United States at (510) 253-0500.

Rockridge Press publishes its books in a variety of electronic and print formats. Some content that appears in print may not be available in electronic books, and vice versa.

TRADEMARKS: Rockridge Press and the Rockridge Press logo are trademarks or registered trademarks of Callisto Media Inc. and/or its affiliates, in the United States and other countries, and may not be used without written permission. All other trademarks are the property of their respective owners. Rockridge Press is not associated with any product or vendor mentioned in this book.

Interior and Cover Designer: Richard Tapp
Art Producer: Janice Ackerman
Editor: Justin Hartung
Production Editor: Ruth Sakata Corley
Production Manager: Riley Hoffman

Photography: ii: ©Darren Muir; vi: ©Darren Muir; viii: ©Martí Sans/Stocksy United: x: ©Darren Muir; p. 16: ©Jeff Wasserman/Stocky United; p. 30: ©Susan Brooks-Dammann; p. 42: ©Nataša Mandić/Stocksy United; p. 54: ©Andrew Cebulka/Stocksy United; p. 74: ©Cameron Whitman/Stocksy United; p. 94: ©Hélène Dujardin; p. 112: Dobránska Renáta/Stocksy United

Illustrated Fire Icon: ©Maxim Kulikov / The Noun Project

ISBN: Print 978-1-63807-310-9
eBook 978-1-63807-215-7
R0

To my mother and sister, who push me to be the best version of myself every day.

Sweet Potato Fries

PAGE 38

Contents

Introduction

Learning to cook can be intimidating for just about anyone. And many guys, especially college guys, tend to think that cooking is either boring or just not worth their time. However, for those who are living on their own for the first time, figuring out how to feed yourself (without food delivery) is very important. When I left for college for the first time, I was just like you. I knew I wanted to cook for myself and maybe some friends, but I had no idea where to start. I needed to find the right place for realistic recipes that actually fit a college lifestyle.

Whether you have never set foot in the kitchen or can already make a complete dinner, this cookbook will give you a wide variety of recipes to keep your meals healthy, interesting, and most of all, delicious. During my four years in college, I developed a ton of awesome recipes, many of which are included in this book. Whether it's dinner alone, an impressive date-night meal, or a feast for a large group of friends, this book will give you everything you need to be successful.

Having just graduated, I understand that college life is far from typical when it comes to cooking. This book has considered everything that can make meals challenging for students, including a small cooking space, limited time, and especially a restricted budget.

Cooking is an incredible skill to learn, not only because of how much fun it can be but also because you'll discover how to create amazing meals you never thought were possible. I hope this book inspires you to begin your cooking journey, incorporating delicious homemade food into your everyday life.

Chapter 1

THE COLLEGE COOKING GAME PLAN FOR GUYS

Whether you are cooking in your dorm room or a small kitchen, you'll need to start with some basics. This chapter will help you learn some easy cooking techniques. It also includes genius hacks to save you time and energy and a list of ingredient staples to always keep on hand.

WHAT'S COOKING, MAN?

No matter where you live during college, finding good, affordable meals to eat on a consistent basis can be a real struggle. If you are beginning your first semester, you're probably eating at the school cafeteria a lot. It's likely close to where you live and offers a wide variety of options on a daily basis. Or you may be hitting local fast-food joints, which you can now enjoy whenever you want because there are no parents to tell you what to do! All those burritos and burgers that

HOW TO SATISFY YOUR CRAVINGS FOR . . .

Whether it's a healthy breakfast before a workout or a midday snack between classes, this book's recipes have you covered at all times of the day. Here are some of my favorites that always seem to hit the spot.

Something Healthy: Begin your day with simple but delicious Avocado Toast (page 24) or slightly more indulgent Fluffy Greek Yogurt Pancakes (page 23). If you want a little extra boost of fruit, try a healthy and refreshing Recovery Breakfast Smoothie (page 18).

Something Quick: I always like to keep a plastic bag of Dark Chocolate, Nut, and Raisin Trail Mix (page 34) on hand for when I need something to take with me on the go. If you want something slightly more substantial, go for a Classic BLT (page 65).

Something to Help You Recover: After a tough workout, I love having a Berry Protein Shake (page 19) or some Homemade Hummus (page 36), which will give you the protein you need to recover. If you're hurting after a long night out, opt for the Full Sunday Scramble (page 94), a weekend staple that will help you and your friends recover after Saturday night.

Something for Your Sweet Tooth: When you need something to hit that that occasional sweet craving, there is nothing easier or more satisfying than Toaster Oven S'mores (page 118). However, if you want something a little lighter that will also last weeks in the freezer, try a refreshing Raspberry-Mint Sorbet (page 112).

seemed like special-occasion food while living at home can now be enjoyed at any time of the day. That sounds unbelievable, right?

Think again. Over the course of a semester, you might realize that it's a little harder to play pickup basketball. Your bank account that you set up at freshman orientation may be dwindling faster than expected. You may be starting to wonder if the convenience of greasy pizza delivery is really worth the cost, bodily or financially. This is where even the simplest dorm room kitchen can be such a useful addition to your life. If you have access to a stovetop and oven, even better!

By cooking your own meals, you are taking complete control of your eating lifestyle. It will help you be the master of your own life, whether it's saving money, exercising better portion control, or just making sure you're eating healthier foods. While it may seem intimidating at first, if you take it slow and learn from your experiences (including the inevitable minor mistakes), you will begin to realize how easy it can be to make cheap and delicious food.

5 BASIC TECHNIQUES EVERY COLLEGE GUY SHOULD KNOW

When you're getting started cooking, there are a few skills that are essential to learn. Especially when you're making recipes that require little or no cooking, nailing these five skills will go a long way in making your food look and taste great.

1. **Measuring** is the process of determining exactly how much of an ingredient you are going to need. In a kitchen, most ingredients are measured by cup, tablespoon, or teaspoon. For example, a recipe for pancakes might ask for 2 cups of flour while seasoning roasted potatoes could include 1 or 2 tablespoons of salt. Measuring is important when you are first beginning because it gives you a good starting point for what your food should taste like. Once you have an idea of how much of an ingredient to add, you can stop measuring and cook using intuition, which allows you to adjust the seasonings to your own preferences.

2. **Mixing** is the process of incorporating one or more ingredients into each other. This could require blending, beating, or stirring, but the end goal is to always make sure that the two ingredients are thoroughly mixed together. A classic example is the first step of making scrambled eggs. When you crack an egg into a bowl, you are left with the egg yolk and egg white. By using a fork or whisk, you mix together the yolk and white until it becomes one homogenous mixture.

3. **Tossing** is the process of adding some type of seasoning or liquid—such as a dressing, sauce, or marinade—to something else so that it evenly coats it. The most common example of tossing is making a salad. Once you have your greens, vegetables, and protein in a bowl, you want to get everything covered in the dressing you've poured over it. Using tongs or large spoons, lift from the bottom of the mix to the top repeatedly, until the liquid has equally coated all of the ingredients.

4. **Slicing** is the process of cutting an ingredient into even, thin strips. This first thing to know is how to properly hold a knife. Using three fingers (pinky, ring, and middle), grab the handle of the knife so that it is secure in your hand. Your hand should comfortably rest on the handle with your index finger on one side of the blade and your thumb gripping the other side of the blade. It should not be a tight grip and should feel comfortable in your hand. To slice, curl the fingers of your opposite hand so that only your knuckles are showing; this will hold your ingredient as well as guide your knife and protect your fingers while you're cutting. Slice downward on the ingredient to cut into slices or moon- or half-moon–shaped pieces. The recipe for Quick French Onion Soup (page 51) uses plenty of thinly sliced onion, so it's a good one to make for some slicing practice.

5. **Chopping/Dicing** is the process of cutting an ingredient into small pieces. The key is to chop the pieces into roughly equal sizes so that they cook evenly. As an example, we are going to use a peeled garlic clove. Hold your knife the same way you would for slicing. Place the palm of your other hand on top of the knife blade (the blunt part), with the sharp edge perpendicular to the cutting board. Using a rocking motion, slowly begin to cut the ingredient into smaller pieces, alternating between horizontal and vertical cuts until the pieces have reached your desired size.

COOKING LINGO

Tackling any new skill means learning the language. And while you'll be learning new words every day throughout your cooking journey, there are some basics you'll encounter again and again.

Beat: To mix ingredients so fast that you're stirring air into them, resulting in a lighter, fluffier texture. You can either beat by hand or with an electric mixer, although all the recipes in this book can be done by hand.

Boil: To heat a liquid over high heat until it bubbles. You'll know you've reached a boil when the bubbles are large and start to steam.

Chop: To cut an ingredient into ½-inch to 1-inch bite-size pieces. Chop generally means the pieces don't have to be perfectly equal.

Dice: To cut an ingredient into ⅛-inch to ¼-inch pieces. This is for ingredients that are so small, they won't change the texture of a dish.

Fold: To gently mix an ingredient into another ingredient so that it doesn't break when added. Think berries, which can be delicate when incorporated into a batter, or chocolate chips when added to cookie dough.

Marinate: To let an ingredient, generally a protein, rest in a liquid or seasoning before cooking to tenderize it and give it amazing flavor. The longer something marinates, the more flavor it can absorb.

Sauté: To cook an ingredient quickly over high heat in oil or butter.

Sear: To quickly cook large pieces of an ingredient so that it creates a dark, brown crust, adding great flavor to the dish. The key to searing is to wait until the pan is just smoking before adding the item.

Simmer: To bring a liquid to a boil before turning it down to low heat so that only small bubbles form. This is done to either reduce (or thicken) a liquid or to keep something warm.

4 RAMEN HACKS

When people think of dorm room cooking, ramen is often at the top of the list. Instant ramen has become the ultimate college food because it's cheap, delicious, and there are so many great ways to switch it up. Here are some of my favorite hacks to take your ramen packs to the next level.

Add an egg: To add some richness to your ramen, whisk an egg into the broth as it's cooking to make it velvety and smooth. It tastes great and is also an easy way to get some extra protein into your meal.

Add some vegetables: Ramen broth is perfect for sneaking in some veggies that you might have ignored all week, from frozen vegetables like peas or carrots to something fresh like spinach or kale.

Add a slice of cheese: While it may sound a little weird, adding a slice of cheddar or American cheese to the hot broth will create an incredible gooey and cheesy soup. You'll thank me later.

Panfry your noodles: While the easy option is to make noodles and broth, sometimes you don't want all that liquid. Once you cook your noodles, strain them completely and panfry them with some ground meat, chicken, or veggies along with some soy sauce and sesame oil for an easy and delicious noodle dish.

BUILDING BIG FLAVOR

If you've never cooked before, the first thing to understand is that seasoning is the key to better food. While seasoning can take a lot of different forms, basically, it's what your food needs to satisfy your specific tastes.

To start, I recommend using salt in every savory dish you make. Salt is found in so many recipes because it helps food taste like its perfect self. An important thing to remember is that you can always add more seasoning as you go but you can't remove it. While it takes time to understand how much to use, learn by constantly tasting as you cook.

Next, I recommend using some type of fat for most cooked dishes. Whether it is olive oil, butter, or even cooking spray, fat helps food become crispy instead of burning, it can finish a sauce so it becomes smooth and silky, or it can just add some richness.

Beyond these two basics, seasoning is entirely up to you. There is a complete list of my most commonly used spices in the Fridge and Pantry section on page 10. If you prefer something spicy, add some extra red pepper flakes or hot sauce. If you like something a little sweeter, honey or brown sugar can transform savory dishes. The best part of making your own food is that you can make it taste exactly like the food you want to eat.

As a self-taught home cook, I can't tell you how many crazy ideas I've tried in my kitchen, just to see what works. It's part of what makes cooking so much

GENIUS MICROWAVE HACKS

My microwave can do what now?! People tend to think a microwave is just for reheating leftovers or making popcorn on a movie night at home. When you're limited on space and cooking equipment, the microwave can be your best friend. It has many different options that can help make a complete meal or even a dessert. Here are some things you might not know you can use it for:

Microwave lemons or limes to make the most of them. Microwaving softens the fruit and makes it easier to squeeze, so you never have to struggle again.

Soften butter when you don't have time. Instead of letting butter sit out for a long time and waiting for the perfect texture, just microwave it in a bowl for 5 to 10 seconds until soft.

Peel garlic with no fuss. Place a few cloves of garlic in the microwave for 10 seconds and watch how easy it is to pull the cloves out of the skins.

Cook bacon without the mess. On a plate, put a few slices of bacon between two paper towels and microwave for 4 to 7 minutes, or until crisp. No splashing grease, no intense cleanup—just a whole lot of deliciousness.

fun. While a recipe is a great road map, there are still so many different variables while cooking, and you'll need to learn to trust your own instincts. By constantly tasting, innovating, and creating something different from what is exactly written, you will be able to understand what tastes best to you.

TRICKING OUT YOUR COLLEGE KITCHEN

No matter how cramped your space is, you can put together a workstation that lets you create all kinds of meals. You'll just need some basic kitchen tools and staple ingredients.

Essential Tools and Equipment

If you've ever walked into a kitchen store, it can be intimidating to see all the fancy tools and gadgets on display. But you don't need much to get started, and you don't have to spend a ton of money. This essential list of tools should have you covered, no matter what you are making.

Tools

Baking Sheet: Whether you are roasting vegetables or making cookies, you need a solid metal baking sheet. Toaster ovens usually come with one, but you'll need to buy one if you're using an oven.

Can Opener: You'll need this for opening soup, beans, tomatoes, or any other cans in your pantry.

Cutting Board: An absolute must in the kitchen, a cutting board is the easiest way to cut anything while cooking. Using a plate or any ceramic material will destroy it and leave scratch marks. I recommend a medium-size silicone board for easy cleanup.

Knives: A large chef's knife and a small paring knife will help you cut everything you will need for this book's recipes.

Measuring Cups and Spoons: To accurately follow some of these recipes, you're going to need to measure. To start, I recommend a 1-cup, ½-cup, and a set of plastic measuring spoons that are easily kept together on a ring.

Meat Thermometer: If you are worried about eating undercooked chicken or beef, a thermometer is a must. They are supercheap and easy to use, and they'll help you cook any meat to the perfect temperature.

Microwave- and Oven-Safe Bowls: Because mixing bowls are typically not microwave- or oven-safe, a glass bowl can be useful, especially for reheating leftovers.

Mixing Bowls: A staple in the kitchen, a mixing bowl is essential for combining liquids, mixing batters, or tossing vegetables with seasoning before cooking. I would start with a few large and small ones.

Oven Mitts: These are necessary for taking anything out of the oven. I recommend a silicone pair that are great at resisting heat and rarely need to be cleaned.

Plastic Food Storage Containers: These are the best containers for storing leftovers. They're durable, microwave-safe, and come in a variety of sizes. Just make sure they come with airtight lids.

Resealable Plastic Bags: Both large and small bags come in handy often. While large bags are generally used to marinate protein in the refrigerator, small bags are great for snacks on the go.

Saucepot: Typically used for making pasta, a saucepot has two handles. Try to get one with heat-resistant handles so you don't burn yourself when straining pasta.

Silicone Turner Spatula: When making anything small like vegetables or eggs in a saucepan, I use a good heat-resistant spatula that will last a long time and is very easy to clean. A must for everything from pancakes to cookies, it also helps get every last drop of batter out of a bowl.

Skillet: My most-used tool in the kitchen, a 12-inch nonstick skillet can be used to cook just about anything on your hot plate or stovetop.

Tongs: This utensil is perfect for flipping veggies or meat—it's like having a heat-resistant hand!

Equipment

Blender: A blender can be used for much more than just your morning smoothie. They're massive time-savers for things like salsas and sauces. If you're short on space, start with a mini blender.

Hot Plate: If you don't access to a stovetop, this is a must-have. While many schools ban them from use in dorm rooms, they will typically allow them in a communal kitchen.

Microwave: Similarly, if you don't have access to an oven, the next best thing is a microwave. Be sure to check the voltage, as the cooking time might change slightly depending on your model.

Mini Fridge: If you plan on keeping lots of food in your room, a mini fridge is the perfect accessory. It's a great way to store ingredients like dairy, protein, and vegetables, not to mention any leftovers you might want to enjoy the next day.

Shaker Bottle: If you want to make smoothies but don't have a blender, a shaker bottle is a great cheap alternative. Just be sure to clean it on a regular basis, as they can get gross quickly.

Toaster Oven: Anything you can cook in an oven you can just as easily cook in a toaster oven. If you are serious about making some of these recipes but don't have an actual oven, this is a must-have.

Fridge and Pantry

To get ready to make the recipes in this book, you'll want to stock up on a few items for your mini fridge and pantry. To avoid food waste, try to think about how much you'll eat throughout the week. For example, buy a smaller milk carton so that you don't have to throw out half of it. Pantry items don't have to be refrigerated and can last a very long time, so spoilage and waste are less of a problem.

For the Mini Fridge

Butter: If you have a choice, go for unsalted butter. You can always add salt to your dishes as needed.

Condiments: Everyone has their own favorite condiments. Ketchup, mustard, mayonnaise, barbecue sauce, ranch dressing, soy sauce, and hot sauce are always popular choices, but you should stock up on your personal favorites. Most condiments last a long time in the fridge, so stock up on what you think you'll use most frequently.

Eggs: Eggs can be used in a variety of dishes for breakfast, lunch, and dinner. Uncooked eggs can last 3 to 5 weeks in the fridge. If you are low on space, buy them by the half dozen.

Milk: Instead of buying a huge gallon, get a quart of your favorite milk. This will help keep it fresh and reduce waste.

Shredded or Sliced Cheese: Shredded cheese is great for eggs or tacos, while sliced cheese is perfect for a quick sandwich. I prefer shredded Mexican-style cheese and sliced cheddar, but go ahead and buy your favorites.

For the Pantry

Flour: Buy a small bag of all-purpose flour, a key ingredient in many baked desserts.

Olive Oil: Olive oil is a crucial (and healthy) tool for sautéing meat and veggies, roasting ingredients in the oven, or making dressings.

Salt and Pepper: While you can use any salt and pepper, I prefer kosher salt and freshly ground black pepper from a pepper grinder for maximum flavor and freshness.

Seasonings: While these are totally up to you, my most commonly used dried spices are garlic powder, onion powder, cumin, chili powder, red pepper flakes, cayenne pepper, paprika, oregano, and rosemary.

Sugar: Store both granulated and brown sugars in resealable plastic bags or airtight containers to keep out ants and humidity.

STORAGE HACKS

Just because you don't have a designated kitchen area doesn't mean you can't create one. Here are a few storage hacks that will help you make the most of your space.

Buy a rolling utility cart. Get one with three trays, so you can store nonperishables on one level, dishes and utensils on another level, and your microwave and anything you tend to use all the time, like salt and pepper or a paper towel holder, on the top.

Repurpose an over-the-door shoe organizer. It's just the right size for storing nonperishable condiments, canned foods, measuring cups, dish towels, oven mitts, and utensils like tongs and spatulas.

Give that plastic three-drawer organizer new life. Typically used to store clothes or papers, they can be filled with kitchenware and nonperishable food. Because they're plastic, they're easy to wipe clean after any inevitable spills.

MONEY-SAVING TIPS

Shop for small appliances in September. That's when many stores roll out new models, offering steep discounts on items such as mini fridges, toaster ovens, and microwaves.

Reuse ingredients for multiple meals. While not every recipe is going to ask for the exact amount you bought, it gives you an opportunity to reuse that ingredient in multiple meals. By getting creative with these leftover ingredients, you can make more elaborate and delicious meals without spending an extra cent.

Shop at big box stores for nonperishables. Stores such as Walmart, Target, and Costco have great deals on bulk food that will keep for months. If you're able to store it and can eat it over the course of a semester, it can save you a ton of money.

Cook more food than you think you need. It was not until college that I learned the incredible value of leftovers. By making larger portions, you can have dinner *and* lunch the next day for the price of one meal.

Split the cost of seasonings and condiments with your roommate. This strategy is one of the best ways to keep your grocery bill from adding up. Just make sure neither of you plan on using it much more than the other.

FUELING UP

Life in college can get busy very quickly. Whether you are writing a term paper, getting ready for that big intramural game, or recovering from a night out, you can easily forget to eat a solid meal. Protein is crucial because it helps your muscles stay strong while also keeping you fuller for longer. From trail mix to yogurt with granola, you can find protein in so many different types of food.

In college, I would always be sure to keep a carton of eggs in my fridge. Scrambled eggs are cheap, quick, and a great source of protein to start your day. When it comes to lunch, I try to have some type of deli meat at home. Regardless of what type of meat you like, it is the perfect addition to any sandwich or salad, or you can just have it on its own as a snack. After finishing a workout or playing a sport, I like to recover with chocolate milk, a great source of protein and healthy sugar. If you are vegetarian or vegan, I would opt for peanut butter and celery sticks or your favorite type of nuts as another easy but nutritious snack choice.

Regardless of what you enjoy, making sure you eat enough is crucial to a healthy lifestyle in college. It can be so easy to skip a meal and therefore miss out on the energy you need to live your active lifestyle. These easy tips will keep you feeling strong and full and ensure your food choices are helping you live your best life.

THE RECIPES IN THIS BOOK

The recipes in this book have been designed to use as few kitchen gadgets as possible while prioritizing time and money. If you have a skillet, hot plate, chef's knife, and toaster oven, you should be able to make almost everything in this book. In fact, many of the recipes in this book require only a microwave or no cooking at all, making your meals just a little bit easier.

No matter the situation, I want to give you all the tools to make great food. Each recipe is labeled with tags such as 15-Minute (for recipes that can be made in 15 minutes or less), 5-Ingredient (for recipes that require 5 ingredients or fewer, not including salt, pepper, oil, or condiments), One-Pot (for recipes that only involve one vessel), and Worth the Wait (for delicious recipes that take at least 40 minutes), so you'll know exactly what you are getting into. Vegetarian and Vegan recipes are also indicated. Additionally, the recipes include icons indicating what cooking equipment is needed to make it:

Blender

Toaster Oven or Oven

Hot Plate or Stovetop

No-Cook

Microwave

While most of the recipes are designed to make one or two servings, the Feasting with Friends chapter has you covered when you want to impress a big group or cook for a special occasion. If you are looking for vegetarian or vegan options, every chapter in this book has multiple options. By considering time, space, and money, this book simply wants to encourage you to make delicious food on a daily basis and have a great time while doing it.

Vanilla Yogurt and Berries
PAGE 20

BREAKFAST

WORTH THE WAIT

VEGETARIAN

VEGAN

ONE-POT

15-MINUTE

5-INGREDIENT

Recovery Breakfast Smoothie

Serves 1
Prep time: 5 minutes

Whether you spent the night studying, finishing a paper, or partying, this smoothie packs the electrolytes you need to recover. By using frozen fruit, banana, and fresh coconut water, you'll get a great variety of vitamins to leave your body feeling recharged and refreshed. Just throw it all in a blender and enjoy.

1 banana, diced
½ cup frozen pineapple chunks
½ cup frozen mango chunks
1 cup coconut water
1 cup ice

1. Add the banana, pineapple, mango, coconut water, and ice to the blender in the order listed.

2. Blend until smooth.

Variation Tip: You may add or subtract any fruit you like. Use frozen strawberries instead of pineapple and mango for a classic strawberry-banana flavor or include a scoop of protein powder for a few extra calories in the morning.

Berry Protein Shake

Serves 1
Prep time: 5 minutes

After a tough workout, the best way to replenish your body is with protein and some healthy sugar, preferably in the form of fruit. This smoothie is one of the easiest and tastiest ways to recover.

1 banana
1 cup fresh or frozen berries
¾ cup water
1 scoop plant-based protein powder

1. In a blender, combine the banana, berries, water, and protein powder.

2. Blend until smooth and creamy, about 50 seconds. Add a bit more water if you like a thinner smoothie.

Variation Tip: For a non-vegan alternative, use whole milk instead of water and a non-vegan protein powder. The possibilities for this smoothie are endless, so use this as a base and change it up as you see fit.

Vanilla Yogurt and Berries

Serves 1
Prep time: 5 minutes

Yogurt with fruit and granola is the perfect breakfast, because it provides protein, fruit, and carbs—and it tastes good! I love this recipe because you can have it multiple times a week without it getting old.

¾ cup vanilla yogurt
¼ cup frozen berries, thawed
2 tablespoons store-bought granola

1. Scoop half the yogurt into a bowl or mug.

2. Add the berries, followed by 1 tablespoon granola, and then top with the remaining yogurt and granola. Although layering isn't necessary, it looks nice and makes your breakfast a little classier.

Cooking Tip: Most stores will carry individual yogurt cups that contain exactly ¾ cup. To make your life easier, use these cups instead to avoid having to clean a bowl or mug.

WORTH THE WAIT

VEGETARIAN

VEGAN

ONE-POT

15-MINUTE

5-INGREDIENT

Peanut Butter and Banana Overnight Oats

Serves 2
Prep time: 5 minutes, plus 8 hours to chill

Overnight oats are great not only because they're delicious, but also because you can do all the work ahead of time. While dried oats are usually cooked, this recipe soaks the oats overnight and requires only 5 minutes to assemble.

1 cup old-fashioned rolled oats
1 cup milk of choice
1 medium banana, sliced
2 tablespoons peanut butter

1 teaspoon ground cinnamon
¼ teaspoon kosher salt
  (optional, omit if peanut butter
  contains salt)

1. Divide the oats, milk, banana, peanut butter, cinnamon, and salt (if using) between two jars and stir to combine.

2. Seal the jars and refrigerate overnight.

Variation Tip: If you like this recipe as much as I do, you'll find yourself using it often. To change it up, expand your ingredients to include chocolate chips, maple syrup, or chopped nuts. If you're vegetarian or vegan, use a dairy-free milk alternative instead of dairy milk.

WORTH THE WAIT

VEGETARIAN

VEGAN

ONE-POT

15-MINUTE

5-INGREDIENT

Toaster Oven Granola

Serves 2
Prep time: 5 minutes
Cook time: 25 minutes

For those who have never made their own granola, I recommend trying it at least once. By making it yourself, you can control exactly how you want it to taste while excluding any processed fats or sugar. Once you make this, it might be hard to go back to packaged granola.

½ cup cashews
1 cup rolled oats
⅓ cup unsweetened coconut flakes
3 tablespoons maple syrup

2 tablespoons olive oil
¼ cup dried cranberries
⅛ teaspoon kosher salt

1. Preheat the toaster oven to 300°F.

2. Place the cashews in a resealable plastic bag. Tightly seal the bag and, using a big spoon or a book, break the cashews up into bite-size pieces.

3. Transfer the cashew pieces to a medium bowl and add the oats, coconut flakes, maple syrup, olive oil, cranberries, and salt. Stir well to combine.

4. Spread the mixture in an even layer on the toaster oven tray. You may need to bake this in two batches, depending on the size of your oven.

5. Bake for 23 to 25 minutes, or until the granola starts to brown.

6. Let the granola cool until it hardens. Break up the cooled granola and store it in an airtight container.

7. Serve with milk or yogurt and fresh fruit.

> **Variation Tip:** If you have a nut allergy, use some crushed pretzels in place of the cashews. You can also use any dried fruit you like.

VEGAN

WORTH THE WAIT

VEGETARIAN

ONE-POT

15-MINUTE

5-INGREDIENT

Fluffy Greek Yogurt Pancakes

Serves 1
Prep time: 5 minutes
Cook time: 10 minutes

If you are looking for your pancake fix, but don't have the time or want all the extra heaviness of a typical flapjack, this recipe has you covered.

¾ cup 2% plain Greek yogurt
1 large egg
½ cup all-purpose flour
1 teaspoon baking soda
Nonstick cooking spray
3 tablespoons maple syrup

1. In a small bowl, mix the yogurt until smooth. Crack an egg into the yogurt and continue mixing until fully incorporated.

2. In a separate medium bowl, combine the flour and baking soda.

3. Pour the yogurt-egg mixture into the bowl with the dry ingredients and stir to combine.

4. Warm a nonstick skillet over medium heat for 2 minutes. Spray with the cooking spray. The spray will help keep the pancakes from sticking to the pan.

5. Spoon ¼ cup of batter into the skillet to form a pancake. Flip the pancakes once they begin to bubble on the surface, about 2 to 4 minutes, and get a golden color underneath. Cook for another 1 to 2 minutes.

6. Remove the pancakes to a plate once they are golden on both sides. Serve with the maple syrup.

Cooking Tip: Make sure your pan is hot enough so that the batter sizzles when added. This will give you a crispy exterior and fluffy interior. If you don't wait, you'll have a pale pancake that isn't fully cooked in the middle.

WORTH THE WAIT

VEGETARIAN

VEGAN

ONE-POT

15-MINUTE

5-INGREDIENT

WORTH THE WAIT

VEGETARIAN

VEGAN

ONE-POT

15-MINUTE

5-INGREDIENT

Avocado Toast

Serves 2
Prep time: 10 minutes
Cook time: 5 minutes

Avocado toast is just the perfect thing to enjoy for breakfast, lunch, or brunch. Salty, creamy, and most important, very Instagram-friendly, this recipe is hard to beat. Avocado can be quite bland on its own, so make sure it's well seasoned!

2 slices bread of your choice
1 ripe avocado
1 teaspoon freshly squeezed lime juice
½ tablespoon olive oil
½ teaspoon red pepper flakes
1 teaspoon kosher salt
Freshly ground black pepper

1. Toast the bread to your desired darkness.

2. In a medium bowl, mash the avocado with a fork. Add the lime juice, olive oil, and red pepper flakes and mix well.

3. Season the avocado mixture with salt and pepper to taste.

4. Spread the mixture over the toast.

Variation Tip: While avocado toast can be a great snack or light meal, it might not fill you up. For a complete breakfast, top this toast with a fried egg or serve alongside some fruit.

Cacio e Pepe Eggs

Serves 2
Prep time: 5 minutes
Cook time: 10 minutes

Scrambled eggs are easy to make and oh so nutritious. Once you've mastered this classic egg dish, you might want to try something a little more interesting. Although this dish name sounds fancy, it just requires eggs, Parmesan cheese, black pepper, and a little technique.

6 large eggs
1 tablespoon unsalted butter
½ teaspoon kosher salt
1½ teaspoons freshly ground black pepper
¼ cup shredded Parmesan cheese

1. Crack the eggs into a medium bowl and beat with a whisk or fork.

2. Into a cold pan, add the butter, eggs, and salt and then turn the burner up to medium heat. By starting in a cold pan, you'll get a soft scramble without over-cooking the eggs.

3. After 1 minute, begin to mix the eggs using a spatula, scraping along the sides and moving the eggs in a figure eight motion.

4. Cook for 4 to 7 minutes, until the eggs are no longer runny but still soft, then turn off the heat. The eggs will continue to cook after the heat is turned off.

5. Add the pepper and Parmesan and mix until incorporated. Taste for seasoning once more and serve, either on its own or with a side of toast.

Appliance Switch-Up: While this recipe was not designed for a microwave, you could easily make this in a mug. Follow steps 4 and 5 of the Microwave Breakfast Tacos (page 26) recipe to cook the eggs and pick back up with step 5 of this recipe.

WORTH THE WAIT

VEGETARIAN

VEGAN

ONE-POT

15-MINUTE

5-INGREDIENT

Microwave Breakfast Tacos

Serves 1
Prep time: 5 minutes
Cook time: 5 minutes

Loaded with bacon, egg, and cheese and topped with avocado and salsa, a break-fast taco is close to the perfect breakfast food. It's filling, flavorful, and comforting. By simplifying the recipe to take only 10 minutes, it's also never been easier to make.

2 bacon slices, halved
2 corn tortillas
2 large eggs
2 tablespoons milk
Kosher salt
Freshly ground black pepper
½ avocado, pitted and diced
1½ tablespoons shredded Mexican-style cheese blend
Store-bought salsa, for serving

1. Place the bacon halves on a microwave-safe plate lined with paper towels, keeping them just far enough apart that they aren't touching.

2. Microwave for 2 minutes, then check for doneness. Continue to microwave in 30-second intervals until they've reached your desired crispness. Let the bacon cool before crumbling into bite-size pieces.

3. While the bacon cools, spread the tortillas out on a plate and microwave them for 15 to 20 seconds. This will allow them to warm up and soften.

4. Crack the eggs into a mug, add the milk, and whisk with a fork until the texture is consistent. Season lightly with salt and pepper and mix once more.

5. Microwave the eggs for 40 seconds. Remove from the microwave, stir, and microwave for 20 to 30 seconds more, or until the eggs are no longer runny.

6. Spoon the eggs equally on the tortillas. Top with the crumbled bacon, avocado, cheese, and salsa.

Variation Tip: One of the best things about these breakfast tacos is that you can add or subtract any ingredient you like. For vegetarian tacos, skip the bacon and go for black beans instead. If you'd like it a little spicy, add some sliced jalapeños for a kick.

WORTH THE WAIT

VEGETARIAN

VEGAN

ONE-POT

15-MINUTE

5-INGREDIENT

Maple Bacon

Serves 2 to 4
Prep time: 5 minutes
Cook time: 40 minutes

If you are ever feeling a little indulgent and want the perfect breakfast item for a special day, this bacon is for you. By slowly cooking your bacon in the oven, brushing it with a sweet glaze, and letting it crisp, you might discover you never want to go back to regular bacon.

½ pound sliced bacon
2 tablespoons maple syrup
2 tablespoons brown sugar
⅛ teaspoon cayenne pepper
Freshly ground black pepper

1. Line a baking sheet with aluminum foil. Lay out the bacon on the foil and place the pan in the oven. Set the oven temperature to 350°F.

2. Cook the bacon for 20 to 30 minutes, checking after 15 minutes, or until just beginning to brown, then remove from the oven.

3. While the bacon is cooking, prepare the maple glaze. In a small bowl, combine the maple syrup, brown sugar, cayenne pepper, and two grinds of black pepper.

4. Using a spoon, liberally apply the glaze to both sides of the bacon.

5. Return the pan of bacon to the oven and cook for another 5 to 7 minutes, or until the glaze is absorbed and the bacon is crispy.

Appliance Switch-Up: This can easily be done in a toaster oven with a smaller amount of bacon. Just use halve the ingredient amounts in this recipe.

Bruschetta

PAGE 35

SNACKS AND SMALL BITES

WORTH THE WAIT

VEGETARIAN

VEGAN

ONE-POT

15-MINUTE

5-INGREDIENT

No-Bake Energy Balls

Makes 24 balls
Prep time: 10 minutes, plus 2 hours to chill
Cook time: 1 minute

When you're starting to crash in the middle of the afternoon, having a great snack can really help you get through the rest of the day. This recipe combines nuts, chocolate, and cranberries to give you a delicious, healthy snack that will keep you feeling energized and full.

½ cup almond butter
¼ cup brown sugar
¼ teaspoon sea salt
1 cup finely chopped nuts and seeds, such as walnuts, almonds, or sunflower seeds

1 cup finely chopped dried cranberries
1 cup coarsely chopped dark chocolate chips

1. In a small microwave-safe bowl, combine the almond butter, brown sugar, and salt and microwave on high for 30 seconds.

2. Stir the mixture and microwave on high for another 30 seconds, or until the mixture is hot and the brown sugar and salt are fully dissolved.

3. In a medium mixing bowl, combine the nuts, cranberries, and chocolate chips.

4. Pour the hot almond butter mixture into the bowl and stir to combine. The heat from the almond butter will begin to melt the chocolate.

5. Scoop the nut mixture into 1-inch balls and pack them with your hands.

6. Place them on a baking sheet and refrigerate until set, about 2 hours. Store in a covered container in the refrigerator.

Variation Tip: If you don't have brown sugar or prefer something a little lighter, use honey or maple syrup. For a different flavor profile, try adding sweetened coconut flakes.

Apple Chips with Cinnamon Yogurt Dip

Serves 2
Prep time: 5 minutes
Cook time: 50 minutes

Instead of going for something from the vending machine for the 1,000th time, try these apple chips. These baked chips are dipped in a protein-packed yogurt dip to make a truly delicious and healthy snack. If you want a little extra crunch, add your favorite type of chopped nuts to the dip.

1 apple, cored and cut into ⅛-inch-thick slices

1 cup plain Greek yogurt

2 teaspoons maple syrup

½ teaspoon ground cinnamon

½ teaspoon vanilla extract

⅛ teaspoon kosher salt

Chopped nuts (optional)

1. Preheat the toaster oven or oven to 275°F. Line a baking sheet with parchment paper or a baking mat.

2. Spread the apple slices in a single layer on the baking sheet and bake for 50 minutes, or until golden and crispy. Check them after 40 minutes to make sure they're not burning.

3. Cool the chips on a rack. The apples will continue to crisp up as they cool.

4. While the chips are baking, in a small bowl, stir together the yogurt, maple syrup, cinnamon, vanilla, and salt until well mixed.

5. Top the dip with chopped nuts (if using) and serve with the baked apple chips.

Prep Tip: To prevent the apple chips from burning in the oven, use aluminum foil, parchment paper, or a baking mat. This will prevent your room from smelling like burnt chips and save you a ton of time cleaning up.

WORTH THE WAIT

VEGETARIAN

VEGAN

ONE-POT

15-MINUTE

5-INGREDIENT

WORTH THE WAIT

VEGETARIAN

VEGAN

ONE-POT

15-MINUTE

5-INGREDIENT

Dark Chocolate, Nut, and Raisin Trail Mix

Serves 1
Prep time: 5 minutes
Cook time: 10 minutes

One of the best snacks to have on the go is a bag of trail mix. You'll get sweetness from the chocolate chips and raisins and salt and crunch from the nuts—and it's (mostly) healthy. This trail mix will keep you full for longer than a bag of chips and will help with that potential afternoon crash.

¼ cup raw almonds
¼ cup peanuts
¼ cup dark chocolate chips
2 tablespoons raisins

1. Preheat the toaster oven or oven to 350°F.

2. Spread the almonds out on the toaster oven tray. Toast the almonds for 6 to 8 minutes, until dark brown. Flip them halfway through by lightly tossing the tray or using a spatula.

3. Allow the almonds to completely cool before combining them in a bowl with the peanuts, dark chocolate chips, and raisins.

Variation Tip: Trail mix is great because you can add almost anything you want. Chocolate candy, pretzels, or any type of dried fruit will make for a tasty alternative.

Bruschetta

Serves 4
Prep time: 5 minutes
Cook time: 10 minutes

Sometimes the simple things in life are the most delicious. Bruschetta is something that seems super fancy but, in reality, is easy to put together. It's a timeless combination of tomatoes, olive oil, and balsamic vinegar piled on top of crispy bread.

1 pint grape or cherry tomatoes, halved
¼ cup coarsely chopped fresh basil
2 tablespoons balsamic vinegar
Sea salt

Freshly ground black pepper
4 tablespoons extra-virgin olive oil, divided
8 slices crusty baguette
¼ cup grated Parmesan cheese

1. In a small mixing bowl, combine the tomatoes, basil, and balsamic vinegar. Season with salt and pepper to taste. Start with less, as you can always add more if needed. Set aside to allow the flavors to come together.

2. In a large skillet, heat 2 tablespoons of oil over medium heat. Let the oil warm up for 1 minute before adding the bread.

3. Add 4 baguette slices and fry for 2 minutes on each side, or until golden brown. Transfer to a serving platter.

4. Fry the remaining slices in the same manner, using the remaining 2 tablespoons of oil, and transfer to the serving platter.

5. Top each of the bread slices with the tomato-basil mixture, sprinkle with the Parmesan (if using), and serve immediately.

Appliance Switch-Up: If you don't have a hot plate or stovetop, you can easily toast your bread instead of frying it. Just forgo the oil before toasting.

WORTH THE WAIT

VEGETARIAN

VEGAN

ONE-POT

15-MINUTE

5-INGREDIENT

Homemade Hummus

Serves 2
Prep time: 5 minutes

Hummus is very popular because it's healthy, filling, and really delicious. Whether you want to keep it as a snack in your fridge or impress some friends at a party, this recipe comes together quickly and is better than anything you can buy.

¼ cup tahini
2 garlic cloves
2 tablespoons freshly squeezed lemon juice
2 tablespoons olive oil
1 (15-ounce) can chickpeas, drained and rinsed
Water, as needed (optional)
Kosher salt

1. In a blender, combine the tahini, garlic, lemon juice, and olive oil.

2. Pulse until smooth, then add the chickpeas and pulse again until smooth.

3. Add water, 1 tablespoon at a time, pulsing between additions until the hummus reaches your desired consistency.

4. Taste and season with salt.

5. Pour the hummus into a bowl and enjoy with pita bread or your choice of crunchy veggies.

Variation Tip: You can flavor your hummus with almost anything you like. While the original is great, adding avocado or spicy roasted red peppers can bring a big boost of flavor.

Buffalo-Ranch Popcorn

Serves 1
Prep time: 5 minutes
Cook time: 5 minutes

Microwave popcorn is a convenient snack, and you can take it to the next level with just a few extra ingredients. By combining the classic flavors of Buffalo sauce and ranch dressing, this savory popcorn will be sure to get you excited for your next movie night or study session.

1 tablespoon unsalted butter
1 bag microwaveable popcorn
1 tablespoon ranch dressing
¼ cup Buffalo sauce

1. In a medium bowl, microwave the butter for 15 seconds, or until melted. Set it aside.

2. Cook the popcorn according to the instructions on the package.

3. While the popcorn is cooking, add the ranch dressing and Buffalo sauce to the butter and stir.

4. Transfer the popcorn to a large bowl.

5. Drizzle the sauce onto the popcorn and mix to evenly coat.

Variation Tip: I love microwave popcorn because it's so versatile. For a sweet option, microwave some chocolate chips and caramel sauce for an easy movie-night dessert.

WORTH THE WAIT

VEGETARIAN

VEGAN

ONE-POT

15-MINUTE

5-INGREDIENT

Sweet Potato Fries with Chipotle Mayonnaise

Serves 2 to 4
Prep time: 10 minutes
Cook time: 40 minutes

Sweet potato fries are absolutely amazing. They get close to the taste and texture of normal fries, but they're much better for you. By baking them in the oven, you save a tremendous amount of time and cleanup. To make cleanup easier, cover the baking sheet with aluminum foil before cooking.

3 small sweet potatoes, peeled and cut into 1-inch-thick strips
2 tablespoons canola oil
Sea salt
¼ cup mayonnaise

1 tablespoon freshly squeezed lemon juice
1 tablespoon minced chipotle peppers in adobo sauce

1. Preheat the toaster oven or oven to 425°F.

2. Spread the sweet potatoes out on a rimmed baking sheet and drizzle with the oil. Toss gently with your hands to coat the sweet potatoes in the oil. Season with sea salt to taste.

3. Roast for 20 minutes, stirring occasionally to ensure even cooking and to prevent sticking.

4. Cook for an additional 15 to 20 minutes, or until the sweet potatoes are browned on the bottom and soft.

5. Meanwhile, whisk together the mayonnaise, lemon juice, and chipotle peppers in a small bowl. Refrigerate until you're ready to serve.

6. Transfer the cooked sweet potato fries to a serving bowl. Taste and add more salt, if needed, and serve with the chipotle mayonnaise.

Guacamole

Serves 4
Prep time: 20 minutes

Guacamole is one of those things that is always better when you make it at home. With creamy avocado, sweet red onion, lime juice, and spicy jalapeños, this guacamole is good for any occasion, whether it's for a party appetizer, taco night, or just as a snack.

3 avocados, pitted and peeled
¼ cup tightly packed cilantro
1 teaspoon kosher salt
¼ cup freshly squeezed lime juice
½ cup diced red onion
3 tablespoons diced jalapeños

1. In a large bowl, mash the avocados with a fork. Add the cilantro, salt, lime juice, red onion, and jalapeños. Mix well to combine.

2. Because avocados vary in size, taste for seasoning. (Remember, you can always add more of an ingredient but you can't remove it.)

Ingredient Tip: To pit and peel an avocado, cut around the outside using a sharp knife, until the two cuts meet. Then twist the two halves to separate them. To remove the pit, carefully chop your knife blade down onto the pit so it gets stuck. Pick your knife up, remove the pit from the knife, and throw it away. Use a spoon to scoop the flesh out.

WORTH THE WAIT

VEGETARIAN

VEGAN

ONE-POT

15-MINUTE

5-INGREDIENT

WORTH THE WAIT

VEGETARIAN

VEGAN

ONE-POT

15-MINUTE

5-INGREDIENT

Mozzarella Sticks

Serves 4
Prep time: 5 minutes
Cook time: 15 minutes

Everyone loves gooey cheese sticks dipped in delicious tomato sauce. They're usually deep-fried, but for this healthier (and easier-to-prepare) version, they are baked. This will be a go-to recipe for game days or your next cram session.

8 pieces string cheese, halved crosswise
1 large egg, whisked
1 cup herb bread crumbs
1 cup store-bought marinara sauce

1. Preheat the toaster oven or oven to 425°F. Line a rimmed baking sheet with parchment paper.

2. Dip each of the string cheese pieces into the egg and shake off any excess, then roll the cheese in the bread crumbs to coat. Arrange on the baking sheet so that the pieces are not touching.

3. Bake for 15 minutes, or until the cheese is beginning to melt and the bread crumbs are lightly browned.

4. Pour the sauce into a bowl and heat for 30 to 60 seconds in the microwave, until hot.

5. Serve the mozzarella sticks with the marinara sauce for dipping.

Variation Tip: While mozzarella sticks are amazing, this works just as well for zucchini sticks. Just cut them into a similar size, bake until crispy, and enjoy a lighter version of this classic.

Bacon-Wrapped Dates

Serves 4
Prep time: 5 minutes
Cook time: 30 minutes

This simple but delicious appetizer always seems to impress people. Combining smoky bacon, sweet dates, and slightly salty cheese, these are great snacks for date night or a gathering of friends.

8 bacon slices
16 fresh dates, pitted
2 ounces hard cheese, such as Manchego or Parmesan, cut into 16 small pieces

1. Preheat the toaster oven or oven to 325°F.

2. Cut the bacon slices in half so they can easily wrap around the dates.

3. Stuff each date with 1 piece of cheese, closing the date around the filling.

4. Wrap 1 bacon slice around each date, and place seam-side down on a rimmed baking sheet.

5. Bake for 10 minutes, then flip each piece to the other side.

6. Cook for 10 to 20 minutes more, or until the bacon fat has rendered and the bites are just beginning to brown.

Ingredient Tip: Be sure to buy pitted dates. Not only are pits a hassle to eat around, but they also don't allow you to fill the inside with delicious cheese!

Buddha Bowl

PAGE 45

Chapter 4

SALADS AND SOUPS

WORTH THE WAIT

VEGETARIAN

VEGAN

ONE-POT

15-MINUTE

5-INGREDIENT

Sesame-Ginger Chopped Salad

Serves 4
Prep time: 5 minutes

Looking for something a little more exciting than your typical cafeteria salad? This side salad has it all. Healthy cabbage and carrots get a flavor boost from cilantro and scallions and crunch from almonds.

1 (8-ounce) package shredded cabbage and carrots blend
1 cup coarsely chopped fresh cilantro
2 scallions, thinly sliced
½ cup sesame-ginger dressing
¼ cup thinly sliced or slivered almonds

1. In a large mixing bowl, mix the shredded cabbage and carrots, cilantro, and scallions to combine.

2. Drizzle with the sesame-ginger dressing, tossing gently to combine. Make sure the entire salad is coated.

3. Divide between the serving plates and top with the sliced almonds.

Variation Tip: Don't like cilantro? Add fresh basil or mint instead. For something more filling, add tofu, grilled chicken, or grilled salmon to make this a complete meal.

Buddha Bowl

Serves 3 or 4
Prep time: 10 minutes
Cook time: 30 minutes

Buddha bowls get their name because they are so packed with ingredients that they resemble the famous spiritual teacher's belly. This recipe uses chickpeas and quinoa for protein, plus a variety of vegetables.

1 cup chopped green beans or
   snow peas
1 radish, sliced
1 (15-ounce) can chickpeas, drained
   and rinsed
3 tablespoons olive oil

⅛ teaspoon kosher salt, plus more
   for seasoning
1 cup water
½ cup quinoa
¼ cup walnuts, halved
Store-bought dressing of choice,
   for serving

1. Preheat the toaster oven or oven to 450°F.

2. On the toaster oven tray, spread the chickpeas in a single layer. Drizzle the entire baking sheet with the olive oil and season with salt to taste. Roast for 20 minutes.

3. In a small pot, bring the water and ⅛ teaspoon of salt to a boil. Once boiling, add the quinoa and immediately reduce the heat to medium-low. Cook for 15 minutes, or until the quinoa is tender, and fluff with a fork.

4. In a medium bowl, combine the chopped vegetables, quinoa, walnuts, and dressing.

Variation Tip: Vary up your bowl with things like roasted sweet potato, bean sprouts, or couscous, or top with a dollop of Homemade Hummus (page 36).

WORTH THE WAIT

VEGETARIAN

VEGAN

ONE-POT

15-MINUTE

5-INGREDIENT

WORTH THE WAIT

VEGETARIAN

VEGAN

ONE-POT

15-MINUTE

5-INGREDIENT

Caprese Salad

Serves 1
Prep time: 5 minutes

A staple of Italian restaurant menus, this salad combines bright, acidic tomatoes with creamy mozzarella and refreshing basil. Whether you are cooking for a friend or just treating yourself, you really can't go wrong with this one.

1 vine-ripened tomato, sliced
5 ounces fresh mozzarella, sliced
10 fresh basil leaves
2 tablespoons extra-virgin olive oil
Kosher salt
Freshly ground black pepper

1. Top a tomato slice with a mozzarella slice followed by a single basil leaf.

2. Repeat this with another tomato slice, alternating with mozzarella and basil in between each tomato layer.

3. When the stack is complete, drizzle the entire plate with olive oil and season generously with salt and pepper.

Cooking Tip: Because the mozzarella and tomato are unseasoned, you might add more salt than you think. You can also drizzle some balsamic vinegar over top to make this dish really pop.

Chicken-Bacon-Ranch Salad

Serves 2
Prep time: 15 minutes
Cook time: 15 minutes

Is there a better combination than chicken, bacon, and ranch? While it's a classic sandwich flavor combination, it's just as good (and better for you) in this easy-to-make salad.

1 boneless, skinless chicken breast
4 bacon slices
½ head romaine lettuce, chopped
1 pint cherry tomatoes

3 carrots, peeled and cut into coins
1 cucumber, peeled and cut into coins
Ranch dressing, for serving

1. Place the chicken in a saucepan, add enough water to cover, and bring to a boil over high heat. Reduce the heat to medium-low and cover the pan with a lid. Simmer for about 15 minutes, until the chicken is no longer pink when you cut into it with a knife. If you have a meat thermometer, make sure the internal temperature is 165°F.

2. Transfer the chicken to a plate and let it cool. Using two forks, shred the meat into small pieces.

3. While the chicken cooks, place the bacon on a microwave-safe plate lined with paper towels, keeping the slices just far enough apart that they aren't touching. Microwave for 4 minutes. Check for doneness and continue to microwave in 20-second intervals until you've reached your desired crispness. Chop the bacon.

4. Place the romaine lettuce in a large bowl and top with the chicken, bacon, tomatoes, carrots, and cucumber. Drizzle with ranch dressing.

Ingredient Tip: While boiled chicken is great for shredding, some people prefer their chicken sautéed. Cook the chicken in a skillet with a little olive oil and cut into strips for a slightly different texture and flavor.

WORTH THE WAIT

VEGETARIAN

VEGAN

ONE-POT

15-MINUTE

5-INGREDIENT

Colombian Chicken Salad

Serves 2 to 4
Prep time: 15 minutes
Cook time: 30 minutes

Some people have a hang-up about mayonnaise-based salads. This chicken salad recipe will change their mind. Serve it on some toast or in a taco shell and be amazed.

1½ pounds boneless, skinless
   chicken breasts
3 tablespoons salt
½ red onion, diced
1 jalapeño, diced
1 avocado, diced

½ cup mayonnaise
Juice of 1 lime
½ tablespoon garlic powder
1 tablespoon olive oil
Kosher salt
Freshly ground black pepper

1. Add the chicken and salt to a pot of cold water and bring to a boil.

2. Boil for about 20 to 25 minutes, or until the chicken is completely cooked through and the internal temperature has reached 165°F. Set aside and let cool.

3. Once cooled, shred the chicken completely with two forks.

4. In a medium bowl, add the shredded chicken, red onion, jalapeño, avocado, and mayonnaise.

5. Season the mixture with the lime juice, garlic powder, olive oil, and salt and pepper to taste.

6. Serve on a piece of toast or in a taco shell.

Appliance Switch-Up: If you don't have a hot plate or stove, you can buy rotisserie chicken and shred it at home. Just make sure to taste it before seasoning and adjust the rest of the spices as needed.

Gazpacho

Serves 4
Prep time: 10 minutes, plus 3 hours to chill
Cook time: 5 minutes

Sometimes it's just too hot outside for a hot bowl of soup. Enter this easy gazpacho. While cold soup is not for everyone, this recipe may convert them. A delicious blend of vegetables and spices, it's as refreshing as it is delicious.

4 medium tomatoes, cut into chunks
½ cup diced cucumber
1 red onion, peeled and quartered
1 red bell pepper, halved and cored
1 jalapeño, deseeded
2 large garlic cloves

Juice of 1 lime
¼ cup olive oil
1 teaspoon dried basil
1 teaspoon cumin, divided
Kosher salt
Freshly ground black pepper

1. Combine the tomatoes, cucumber, onion, bell pepper, jalapeño, garlic, lime juice, olive oil, basil, and ½ teaspoon of cumin in a blender.

2. Blend on high for 1 to 2 minutes, or until smooth.

3. Add the remaining ½ teaspoon of cumin, as well as a generous amount of salt and pepper to taste.

4. Blend one more time to make sure there are no lumps or chunks and the mixture is smooth.

5. Refrigerate for a few hours before serving.

Cooking Tip: To take this soup to the next level, consider including some additional toppings before serving. You can add fresh basil, croutons, or even a splash of olive oil on top.

Creamy Tomato Soup

Serves 2
Prep time: 5 minutes
Cook time: 35 minutes

Making your own tomato soup might seem a little extra, because it's easy to buy a can. However, what most people don't realize is how much salt and unnecessary fat come in a typical can of tomato soup. By cooking it yourself, you'll have a much healthier and tastier soup.

2 tablespoons unsalted butter
½ yellow onion, diced
1 (28-ounce) can crushed tomatoes, drained
1 cup low-sodium vegetable broth
¼ teaspoon kosher salt
½ teaspoon freshly ground black pepper

1. In a medium saucepan over medium heat, melt the butter.

2. Add the onion and cook until tender, about 2 to 3 minutes.

3. Increase the heat to medium-high, add the tomatoes, vegetable broth, salt, and pepper, and bring the soup to a boil. Reduce the heat to medium-low and let simmer, uncovered, for about 30 minutes.

4. Carefully transfer the soup to a blender, making sure to fill it no more than half-way. Cover with the lid and blend until smooth.

Prep Tip: If you have extra soup that you don't plan on eating right away, store it in a container with an airtight lid and put it in the freezer. It will taste just as good whenever you're craving homemade soup and don't feel like cooking.

Quick French Onion Soup

Serves 2
Prep time: 5 minutes
Cook time: 10 minutes

This soup is like a big hug in a bowl. The combination of caramelized onions, toast, and gooey cheese creates the ultimate comfort food. You'll be surprised how much flavor you can get cooking in a microwave in such a short amount of time.

1 tablespoon unsalted butter
½ Vidalia onion, cut into slices
2 cups low-sodium beef broth
¼ cup water
¼ teaspoon garlic powder

Kosher salt
Freshly ground black pepper
1 baguette, cut into pieces
2 slices Swiss or provolone cheese

1. Place the butter in a large microwave-safe bowl and microwave for 20 to 25 seconds, or until melted. Add the onion and stir to coat.

2. Place a paper towel on top of the bowl to prevent splattering and microwave for 5 to 7 minutes, stirring halfway through, until the onion is just beginning to get brown.

3. Add the beef broth, water, and garlic powder. Cover the bowl with the paper towel again and microwave for 3 more minutes. Season with salt and pepper to taste.

4. Ladle the soup into 2 bowls. Top with the bread pieces and cheese. Let sit for 2 minutes, until the bread absorbs the broth and the cheese melts.

Cooking Tip: If you have a toaster oven and a small oven-safe bowl, you can finish your soup off in a more traditional style. Top your soup with the baguette and cheese and then broil it for a few minutes, until the cheese is bubbly and browned.

WORTH THE WAIT

VEGETARIAN

VEGAN

ONE-POT

15-MINUTE

5-INGREDIENT

WORTH THE WAIT

VEGETARIAN

VEGAN

ONE-POT

15-MINUTE

5-INGREDIENT

Easy Chicken Noodle Soup

Serves 1
Prep time: 10 minutes
Cook time: 15 minutes

Chicken noodle soup seems to remind people of home. If you are starting to feel a little under the weather, chicken noodle soup has been scientifically proven to help you recover. It may not be quite as good as a parent taking care of you, but it's a close second.

1 tablespoon olive oil
2 tablespoons diced onion
1 celery stalk, diced
1 carrot, sliced
3 cups chicken broth
½ cup cooked chicken, chopped
⅛ teaspoon dried basil

⅛ teaspoon dried thyme
⅛ teaspoon dried oregano
Kosher salt
Freshly ground black pepper
½ cup egg noodles or pasta of
  your choice

1. In a large saucepan, heat the olive oil over medium-high heat. Add the onion, celery, and carrot and cook for 3 to 4 minutes, or until the onions are translucent.

2. Add the chicken broth, chicken, basil, thyme, and oregano, season with salt and pepper to taste, and turn up to high heat until boiling.

3. Add the egg noodles and boil for 10 minutes, or until cooked through, and serve.

Ingredient Tip: When it comes to a homemade soup, seasoning is crucial. While this recipe is a good base, be sure to taste it as you cook as you might need to add more seasonings. Just note that the flavors will become more intense the longer you cook it.

Tortilla Soup

Serves 4
Prep time: 10 minutes
Cook time: 15 minutes

I love this recipe, because it shows how much flavor you can get from just a handful of ingredients. With tomatoes, chicken, and beans, it's a complete meal in a bowl.

3 cups low-sodium chicken broth
1 (14.5-ounce) can fire-roasted tomatoes, drained
1 boneless, skinless chicken breast, cut into 1-inch pieces
1 (15-ounce) can black beans, drained and rinsed

Juice of 1 lime
Kosher salt
Freshly ground black pepper
½ cup shredded Monterey Jack or pepper Jack cheese, for serving
Crushed tortilla chips, for serving

1. In a medium saucepan over medium-high heat, stir together the chicken broth and tomatoes and bring to a boil.

2. Once it's boiling, add the chicken and black beans to the pan. Cover the pan, reduce the heat to medium-low, and simmer for 10 to 12 minutes, until the chicken is no longer pink when you cut into it with a knife. If you're unsure if its fully cooked, check the chicken with a meat thermometer to make sure the internal temperature has reached 165°F.

3. Stir in the lime juice and season with salt and pepper.

4. Ladle the soup into bowls and garnish with the cheese and crushed tortilla chips.

Variation Tip: This recipe can easily be made vegetarian or vegan. Replace the chicken broth with vegetable broth, replace the chicken with some tofu or quinoa, and skip the cheese.

Cuban Sandwich

PAGE 68

SANDWICHES AND HANDHELDS

WORTH THE WAIT

VEGETARIAN

VEGAN

ONE-POT

15-MINUTE

5-INGREDIENT

Vegetarian Banh Mi

Serves 2
Prep time: 10 minutes, plus
30 minutes to marinate
Cook time: 10 minutes

A banh mi is a popular Vietnamese sandwich, typically made with grilled pork and pickled vegetables on a baguette. When you replace the pork with some marinated tofu, you still get the amazing flavor without the heaviness of meat.

1 tablespoon grapeseed oil, plus extra for greasing
1 tablespoon soy sauce
1 teaspoon honey or maple syrup
1 (1-inch) piece fresh ginger, grated (or 1¼ teaspoons ground ginger)
½ (14-ounce) block extra-firm tofu, drained, pressed, and sliced into 4 pieces
2 (6-inch) baguettes, cut into 4 slices (or 2 sandwich rolls, halved)
¼ cup mayonnaise
1 cup pickled carrots, jalapeños, or other vegetables
¼ cup fresh cilantro

1. In a small bowl, whisk together the oil, soy sauce, honey, and ginger and transfer the mixture to a medium sealable plastic or silicone bag.

2. Add the tofu pieces to the bag, seal it, and let them marinate for at least 30 minutes or in the refrigerator overnight.

3. Lightly oil a skillet and preheat it over medium heat.

4. Arrange the tofu in the skillet in a single layer and cook for 4 minutes, or until the pieces easily separate from the pan.

5. Flip the tofu pieces over and cook for an additional 4 minutes, or until they again easily separate from the pan.

6. Coat the inside of the baguette slices with the mayonnaise. Divide the tofu between 2 of the baguette slices and top with the pickled vegetables and cilantro. Top each with a second slice of bread and enjoy.

Ingredient Tip: While you can find jarred pickled vegetables in most stores, it is fairly easy to make your own at home. Heat 1 cup of vinegar, 1 cup of water, 1 teaspoon of salt, and 1 teaspoon of granulated sugar in a saucepan and bring to a boil. Add the vegetables you want to pickle to a mason jar. Once the sugar and salt are dissolved, pour the brine into the mason jar over the vegetables and refrigerate for at least 24 hours and up to 1 week.

WORTH THE WAIT

VEGETARIAN

VEGAN

ONE-POT

15-MINUTE

5-INGREDIENT

Falafel-Stuffed Pita

Serves 2
Prep time: 15 minutes
Cook time: 30 minutes

Falafel is a staple dish throughout the Middle East. It's typically made with chickpeas, formed into patties, deep-fried, and served in a pita with tahini (sesame seed paste) and fresh veggies. This variation is both easier to make and significantly healthier than the traditional method.

¼ cup grapeseed oil
1 (15-ounce) can chickpeas, drained and rinsed well
½ cup whole wheat flour
½ cup diced red onion
½ cup shredded carrot
1 tablespoon ground cumin
¼ teaspoon kosher salt
⅛ teaspoon freshly ground black pepper

2 pita flatbreads, 1 inch trimmed off the top of each, warmed
½ cup sliced cucumber
½ cup sliced tomato
½ cup sliced red onion
¼ cup tahini
2 tablespoons freshly squeezed lemon juice

1. Preheat the oven to 375°F and pour the oil onto a rimmed baking sheet. Tilt the baking sheet until the surface is evenly coated with the oil.

2. Put the chickpeas, flour, diced red onion, carrot, cumin, salt, and pepper in a food processor and process for 1 minute, or until a thick paste forms.

3. Use your hands to roll the mixture into 2-tablespoon balls and transfer them to the baking sheet, arranging them in a single layer.

4. Bake the falafel for 30 minutes, carefully flipping them halfway through; be careful because the falafel and oil on the baking sheet will be very hot.

5. Remove the pan from the oven and let the falafel cool enough to handle, about 15 minutes.

6. Open the pockets of the pita breads and place half the baked falafel into each.

7. Fill each pita bread with some cucumber, tomato, sliced red onion, tahini, and lemon juice and serve.

Variation Tip: Instead of tahini, try topping this sandwich with Homemade Hummus (page 36). Just line the inside of the pita with a big scoop.

WORTH THE WAIT

VEGETARIAN

VEGAN

ONE-POT

15-MINUTE

5-INGREDIENT

Mushroom Cheesesteak

Serves 2
Prep time: 5 minutes
Cook time: 15 minutes

The classic Philly cheesesteak is made with thinly sliced rib eye and Cheez Whiz piled on a giant hoagie roll. The one problem with this hearty sandwich: After eating three bites, you'll need a long nap. By replacing the meat with some seasoned mushrooms, you can enjoy all the flavor without losing valuable hours from your day.

1 tablespoon grapeseed oil
½ sweet onion, thinly sliced
2 fresh portobello mushroom caps, cut into ¼-inch slices
½ teaspoon dried rosemary (optional)
¼ teaspoon cayenne pepper (optional)
¼ teaspoon kosher salt
⅛ teaspoon freshly ground black pepper
2 hoagie rolls, halved
2 slices provolone cheese

1. Preheat the toaster oven or oven to 400°F. Line a baking sheet with parchment paper.

2. Heat the grapeseed oil in a large skillet over medium heat.

3. Once the oil is shiny, add the onion and cook for 3 minutes, or until translucent.

4. Turn the skillet up to high heat, add the mushrooms, rosemary (if using), cayenne (if using), salt, and pepper and cook for 5 to 7 minutes, or until the mushrooms begin to darken in color.

5. Arrange the hoagie rolls, cut-side up, on the baking sheet. Evenly divide the mushroom mixture between two of the hoagie halves and top with the provolone cheese.

6. Bake until the cheese is melted, about 5 minutes. Place the hoagie halves on top of the mushroom-cheese mixture and serve.

Ingredient Tip: Mushrooms can be tricky to cook because they contain mostly water. Once you add them to the pan, spread them out evenly throughout the pan while moving them as little as possible. This will help them brown instead of steam.

Tomato and Pesto Grilled Cheese

Serves 1
Prep time: 5 minutes
Cook time: 10 minutes

While everyone has fond memories of eating grilled cheese as a child, those sandwiches aren't always as good as we remember and, frankly, can get a little boring after a while. This improved version gets a bright kick from tomato and pesto and won't leave you feeling weighed down after lunch.

2 tablespoons store-bought pesto
2 slices sourdough (or other thick bread)
2 thin slices tomato
Kosher salt
Freshly ground black pepper
2 slices cheddar cheese
1 to 2 tablespoons unsalted butter, for toasting bread

1. Spread the pesto on one side of each slice of bread. Top with tomato and sprinkle with salt and pepper to taste. Top with cheese and the other slice of bread, pesto-side down.

2. Spread the butter on the outside surface of each slice.

3. Place a skillet over medium heat. Once hot, add the sandwich to the pan. You can test to see if it's hot enough by flicking water onto the pan. If it sizzles, it's ready.

4. Cook for 3 to 4 minutes. Flip and cook an additional 3 to 4 minutes, or until crispy on both sides.

Appliance Switch-Up: If you only have a toaster oven, assemble the sandwich the exact same way but first toast it open-faced until the cheese begins to melt. Then assemble the sandwich and toast some more to crisp the outside.

WORTH THE WAIT

VEGETARIAN

VEGAN

ONE-POT

15-MINUTE

5-INGREDIENT

Fully Loaded Quesadilla

Serves 1
Prep time: 5 minutes
Cook time: 5 minutes

Everyone loves a quesadilla because it's easy, quick, and hits the spot. Going beyond the usual tortilla and cheese, this recipe gets supersized by adding black beans, jalapeños, and red bell peppers, making it a complete meal.

1 teaspoon canola or vegetable oil
1 large tortilla
⅓ cup shredded cheddar cheese
2 tablespoons canned black beans
2 tablespoons pickled jalapeños
2 tablespoons finely diced red bell pepper

1. In a skillet over medium heat, heat the oil for 1 minute. Place the tortilla in the hot skillet and place the cheese, beans, jalapeños, and bell pepper on ½ of the tortilla.

2. With a spatula, fold the empty ½ of the tortilla over to cover the filling. Press down firmly with the spatula to let the melting cheese adhere to the top of the tortilla. Hold for 1 minute.

3. After cooking for 3 minutes, use the spatula to flip the quesadilla over, then let it cook for 2 more minutes.

4. Slide the quesadilla onto a cutting board and cut it into thirds or quarters.

> **Ingredient Tip:** For an even cheesier quesadilla, right before flipping to the second side, add some cheese straight into the bottom of the pan. It will crisp up, stick to the tortilla, and add some amazing crunch.

WORTH THE WAIT

VEGETARIAN

VEGAN

ONE-POT

15-MINUTE

5-INGREDIENT

WORTH THE WAIT

VEGETARIAN

VEGAN

ONE-POT

15-MINUTE

5-INGREDIENT

Pizza Bagels

Serves 1
Prep time: 5 minutes
Cook time: 10 minutes

If you ever had pizza bagels as a kid, you know how good these can be. Instead of going through the hassle of making an actual pizza, you can just add pizza toppings to a plain bagel and enjoy. Perfect for a quick lunch or snack, this will bring you right back to your after-school snack days.

1 plain bagel, sliced
½ cup tomato sauce
1 cup shredded mozzarella cheese
10 slices pepperoni

1. Preheat the toaster oven to 350°F.

2. Line the toaster oven tray with aluminum foil and place the bagel slices faceup on it.

3. Spread the sauce on each bagel.

4. Evenly top both bagel slices with the mozzarella cheese. Add the pepperoni on top.

5. Bake in the toaster oven for 7 to 10 minutes, until the cheese is melted and golden, and serve.

Variation Tip: Use those leftovers in your fridge as additional toppings. Any type of cooked vegetable or protein can make a delicious pizza topping.

Classic BLT

Serves 1
Prep time: 5 minutes
Cook time: 5 minutes

The BLT has always been a go-to sandwich because of its simplicity. By "hiding" the lettuce and tomato with some crispy, salty bacon, you get everything you want in a lunch. This comes together in less than 10 minutes, making sure your lunch will be both delicious and nutritious.

2 slices whole wheat bread
1 tablespoon mayonnaise
2 bacon slices
2 lettuce leaves
2 (½-inch-thick) slices tomato

1. Toast the bread.

2. Spread the mayonnaise across one slice of toast.

3. Lay a paper towel on a microwave-safe plate and place the bacon on top. Microwave for 4 minutes, or until crispy.

4. Assemble the BLT by stacking the bacon, lettuce, and tomato between both slices of toast and serve.

> **Variation Tip:** If this BLT isn't interesting enough, add some other classic sandwich toppings. Depending on how I'm feeling, I add avocado, hot sauce, or even everything bagel seasoning.

WORTH THE WAIT

VEGETARIAN

VEGAN

ONE-POT

15-MINUTE

5-INGREDIENT

Tuna Salad Sandwich

Serves 1
Prep time: 5 minutes

If you're looking for an easy dorm-friendly lunch, look no further than this tuna salad sandwich. This recipe requires no cooking, is full of protein, and is easy to take on the go. Tuna can easily be stored in your pantry for those days when you just don't know what to make.

1 (5-ounce) can tuna, drained
2 tablespoons mayonnaise
½ cup chopped celery
1 tablespoon diced red onion
1 teaspoon garlic powder
Kosher salt
Freshly ground black pepper
2 slices sourdough bread or other bread

1. In a bowl, combine the tuna, mayonnaise, celery, red onion, and garlic powder and season with salt and pepper to taste. Mix until all ingredients are equally incorporated.

2. Spoon the tuna mixture onto a slice of bread and spread it out evenly.

3. Top with the second slice of bread.

4. Cut in half and enjoy.

Cooking Tip: If you have a toaster or hot plate and prefer a hot sandwich, try to make a tuna melt! It's the same exact sandwich with an added cheese slice and toasted until the cheese is melted.

Turkey Reuben

Serves 1
Prep time: 2 minutes
Cook time: 5 minutes

A Reuben has been a diner classic for as long as I can remember. Who wouldn't want a sandwich with sauerkraut, Thousand Island dressing, and Swiss cheese? Grilled until hot and toasted, this sandwich is satisfying every single time.

¼ cup sauerkraut, drained
1½ teaspoons unsalted butter, at room temperature
2 slices rye bread
1 tablespoon Thousand Island dressing
2 slices Swiss cheese
4 slices smoked turkey

1. Place the sauerkraut in a small microwave-safe bowl and microwave for 30 seconds. Set aside.

2. Spread the butter on one side of each slice of bread. Spread the Thousand Island dressing on the other side of each slice.

3. Place one slice of bread butter-side down on a cutting board. Layer with 1 slice of cheese, the turkey, sauerkraut, and the other slice of cheese.

4. Top with the remaining slice of bread, butter-side up.

5. Heat a skillet over medium heat. Place the sandwich in the skillet and cook for about 3 minutes, until the bread is lightly golden and the cheese has started to melt.

6. Using a spatula, gently flip the sandwich and cook for 2 more minutes, until golden brown on the other side.

Variation Tip: If you don't like turkey, you can easily swap it with any type of meat. The classic substitution is pastrami, but go with whatever you're in the mood for.

WORTH THE WAIT

VEGETARIAN

VEGAN

ONE-POT

15-MINUTE

5-INGREDIENT

Cuban Sandwich

Serves 2
Prep time: 10 minutes
Cook time: 5 minutes

If you've never had a Cuban sandwich, you've really been missing out. Imagine a ham and cheese sandwich but taken up 1,000 levels. By adding roast pork, mustard, and a mojo marinade (usually found in the "international aisle" of the grocery store), it all comes together to make a nearly perfect bite. Instead of taking multiple hours to roast your own pork, most grocery stores carry refrigerated, fully cooked pork. Just reheat it according to the package instructions before using it in this sandwich.

8 ounces shredded store-bought
   roast pork
¼ cup bottled mojo marinade
1 tablespoon unsalted butter, at
   room temperature

4 slices bread of choice
1 tablespoon yellow mustard
4 slices Swiss cheese
4 slices deli ham
Dill pickles, for serving

1. In a medium bowl, toss together the roast pork and mojo marinade. Set aside.

2. Spread the butter on one side of each bread slice. Spread the mustard on the other side.

3. Layer half the cheese over the mustard, then add the ham, marinade-pork mixture, pickles, and the remaining cheese slices. Close the sandwich, mustard-side down.

4. Heat a skillet over medium heat. Place the sandwich in the skillet and cook for about 3 minutes, pressing it down with a spatula or the bottom of a clean skillet, until the cheese is melted.

5. Flip the sandwich and cook for 1 to 2 minutes more, until golden brown.

6. Cut in half and enjoy with dill pickles.

Appliance Switch-Up: If you have a panini press but no hot plate, it can be a great addition to this recipe. It will flatten the sandwich and make the bread extra crispy, a staple when making a traditional Cuban.

Roast Beef Sandwich with Homemade Cheese Sauce

Serves 2
Prep time: 5 minutes
Cook time: 10 minutes

Every once in a while, you just feel the need to pig out. While there is a famous fast-food restaurant that is known for this sandwich, I think you'll notice a clear difference in making it yourself. This sandwich is perfect for a lazy day with a friend.

2 onion rolls, halved horizontally
2 tablespoons unsalted butter, at room temperature, divided
8 ounces sliced deli roast beef
1 tablespoon all-purpose flour
½ cup whole milk
½ cup shredded sharp cheddar cheese
¼ teaspoon chili powder
Kosher salt
Freshly ground black pepper

1. Preheat the toaster oven to 375°F.

2. Spread the insides of the rolls with 1 tablespoon of butter. Divide the roast beef evenly between each roll.

3. Place the rolls and roast beef in the toaster oven to warm, about 3 to 5 minutes.

4. To make the cheese sauce, in a saucepan over medium heat, melt the remaining 1 tablespoon of butter.

WORTH THE WAIT

VEGETARIAN

VEGAN

ONE-POT

15-MINUTE

5-INGREDIENT

5. Once melted, whisk in the flour to create a paste, mixing constantly, for about 30 seconds.

6. Slowly pour in the milk as you continue to whisk, allowing the paste to dissolve into the milk. There should be no lumps.

7. Slowly whisk in the cheese and chili powder until it has fully melted and creates a smooth sauce. Taste for seasoning and add salt and pepper as needed.

8. Remove the rolls from the toaster oven and drizzle the cheese sauce over the roast beef. Top with the remaining roll halves and serve.

Ingredient Tip: This recipe is a great base for making any type of cheese sauce. Once you combine the butter, flour, and milk, you can use any cheese you like to make all types of variations.

WORTH THE WAIT

VEGETARIAN

VEGAN

ONE-POT

15-MINUTE

5-INGREDIENT

Buffalo Chicken Wrap

Serves 1
Prep time: 5 minutes

As far as on-the-go lunches come, this has to be one of my favorites. It uses already cooked chicken, amplified by coating it in Buffalo sauce and ranch dressing, and throws it all in a tortilla for easy portable eating. It doesn't get much better than that. Note: Many grocery stores carry precooked whole chickens, which are perfect for this recipe as well as other sandwiches and salads.

1 cup diced precooked chicken
¼ cup Buffalo sauce
1 (10-inch) whole wheat tortilla
2 tablespoons ranch dressing
1 cup shredded iceberg lettuce

1. In a medium bowl, mix the chicken with the Buffalo sauce until it is evenly coated.

2. Arrange the chicken mixture in the center of the tortilla. Drizzle the ranch dressing on top.

3. Evenly top the chicken with the lettuce.

4. Fold one of the long ends of the tortilla over the filling. Tuck in the two short sides over the existing fold. While keeping the contents tight in the tortilla, continue rolling until fully wrapped.

Variation Tip: For a vegetarian spin on this classic, skip the chicken and opt for a roasted vegetable like mushrooms or cauliflower. For a fresh and colorful addition, include some sliced avocado.

Juicy Turkey Meatballs

PAGE 86

SOLO MEALS

WORTH THE WAIT

VEGETARIAN

VEGAN

ONE-POT

15-MINUTE

5-INGREDIENT

Easy Coconut Curry

Serves 1
Prep time: 5 minutes
Cook time: 10 minutes

You need to add some curry into your recipe rotation. Rice is a great addition to many college meals because it's so cheap and can last forever in your pantry. This recipe combines a handful of ingredients in an incredibly short amount of time to give you a flavorful, vegan dinner choice.

½ cup uncooked white rice
½ cup water
½ teaspoon curry powder
⅓ cup canned coconut milk

2 tablespoons finely diced red
  bell pepper
1 teaspoon chopped fresh cilantro
1 lime wedge
Kosher salt

1. Pour the rice and water into a microwave-safe bowl and cover with a microwave-safe lid.

2. Microwave on high for 5 minutes. Check that the rice is cooked. If it's not cooked, cook for another minute and check again. Continue checking and cooking until the rice is fluffy.

3. In a separate bowl, whisk together the curry powder and coconut milk, then stir in the bell pepper and cilantro.

4. When the rice is cooked, pour the curry over the top of the rice and squeeze in the lime juice. Season with salt, stir well, and enjoy.

Ingredient Tip: If you have a little extra time and want amazing rice, I recommend rinsing it in a strainer before cooking. Naturally, rice has a ton of starch that can make it gummy or dry. By washing it a couple times until the water runs clear, you will end up with fluffy and moist rice.

Vegan Pad Thai

Serves 1
Prep time: 5 minutes
Cook time: 5 minutes

Rice noodles are like a lighter, softer version of spaghetti. Toss them in peanut sauce (which can easily be found in the "international aisle" of most grocery stores), lime juice, and some fresh toppings, and you've got one of the easiest gourmet meals around.

4 ounces rice noodles
1 tablespoon freshly squeezed
   lime juice
2 tablespoons store-bought
   peanut sauce
¼ bell pepper, any color,
   thinly sliced

¼ cup bean sprouts
1 scallion, white and light green
   parts only, sliced
Chopped fresh cilantro, for garnish
   (optional)
Chopped roasted peanuts, for garnish (optional)

1. Cook the noodles according to package instructions. Drain and rinse with cold water.

2. In a medium bowl, whisk together the lime juice and peanut sauce until fully combined.

3. Add the noodles, bell pepper, sprouts, and scallion and toss to combine.

4. Garnish with the cilantro and peanuts (if using).

Cooking Tip: It is crucial to not overcook your rice noodles. They will continue to cook until they are rinsed and can get gummy very quickly. Rice noodles cook much quicker than a typical box of pasta, so follow the instructions on the box and stir as you go to ensure even cooking.

WORTH THE WAIT

VEGETARIAN

VEGAN

ONE-POT

15-MINUTE

5-INGREDIENT

Sesame-Lime Tofu

Serves 1
Prep time: 10 minutes
Cook time: 10 minutes

Tofu gets a bad reputation for being bland. Those people, I say, just don't know how to cook tofu. By cooking it in sesame oil, lime juice, and soy sauce, you just might begin to have a few more meatless meals.

5 to 6 ounces firm or extra-firm tofu
1 tablespoon toasted sesame oil
1 tablespoon freshly squeezed
  lime juice

1 tablespoon soy sauce
1 scallion, white and light green
  parts only, chopped, plus more
  for serving

1. Press your tofu: Place the block of tofu between several layers of paper towels and place a heavy pan (or other heavy object) on top. Let stand for 10 minutes.

2. Discard the paper towels and cut the tofu into cubes.

3. Heat the sesame oil in a skillet over medium-high heat until hot. Add the tofu cubes and cook for 2 to 3 minutes, until they are lightly golden brown.

4. Flip and cook for 2 to 3 more minutes, until the other side also has some nice color.

5. Drizzle in the lime juice and soy sauce, and sprinkle scallion all over the pan. The liquid will begin to thicken as soon as you add it.

6. Cook the tofu for 1 to 2 more minutes, until the sauce coats all the pieces. If it begins to smell like it is burning, remove the pan from the heat immediately.

7. Serve topped with additional chopped scallion.

Cooking Tip: While pressing the tofu may seem like an unnecessary step, it is more important than you think. Because tofu has so much water in it, if you do not dry it, the tofu will never crisp up in the pan, no matter how long you cook it.

French Bread Pizza

Serves 1
Prep time: 5 minutes
Cook time: 10 minutes

It's a well-known rule: When you're in college, you're going to crave pizza sometimes. While frozen pizza or delivery pizza is the easy option, there's no fun in that. In fewer than 15 minutes, you can have a personal pizza, with any toppings you want, for a fraction of the price. Perfect for a simple weeknight dinner while studying or a quick meal after a night out.

½ loaf French bread
¼ cup pizza sauce or marinara sauce

¾ cup shredded mozzarella cheese
4 fresh basil leaves (optional)

1. Preheat the toaster oven or oven to 400°F.

2. Cut the French bread in half lengthwise and place both halves cut-side up on your baking tray.

3. Top each with the pizza sauce, mozzarella cheese, and basil (if using).

4. Bake for 10 minutes, or until the cheese is lightly browned, and serve.

Variation Tip: If you don't have a loaf of French bread, you can get creative with your base. Try a 10-inch tortilla, a soft taco shell, or even some pita bread. Just adjust the cook time using your best judgment.

WORTH THE WAIT

VEGETARIAN

VEGAN

ONE-POT

15-MINUTE

5-INGREDIENT

WORTH THE WAIT

VEGETARIAN

VEGAN

ONE-POT

15-MINUTE

5-INGREDIENT

Toaster Oven Eggplant Parm

Serves 1 or 2
Prep time: 10 minutes, plus 30 minutes
for eggplant to drain
Cook time: 20 minutes

Eggplant Parmesan is truly amazing when done correctly. With crispy eggplant, tangy tomato sauce, and gooey cheese, it's perfect as a classy appetizer or a week-night meal alongside some pasta. By salting the eggplant ahead of time to draw out the moisture, we get perfectly crisp eggplant without the hassle of frying.

1 eggplant
Kosher salt
1 large egg, beaten
½ cup panko bread crumbs
2 cups marinara sauce
1 cup shredded mozzarella, divided
2 tablespoons grated Parmesan cheese, divided

1. Cut the eggplant horizontally into ¼-inch circular slices. Sweat the eggplant by sprinkling salt onto each side of the slices and placing them in a colander. After 30 minutes, rinse the salt off and dry with paper towels.

2. Preheat the toaster oven or oven to 400°F and line a baking tray with aluminum foil.

3. Set up a dipping station with one bowl with the beaten egg and one bowl with the bread crumbs side by side.

4. One at a time, dip each eggplant slice into the beaten egg and then into the bread crumbs so each slice is completely covered. Place the slices on the toaster oven tray.

5. Bake for 10 minutes, flipping after 5 minutes. Remove the pan from the toaster oven and lower the temperature to 350°F. Depending on the size of the toaster oven and eggplant, you may need to cook the slices in two batches.

6. Cover the top of each slice with 2 to 3 tablespoons of marinara sauce, 1 tablespoon of mozzarella, and a pinch of Parmesan.

7. Bake in the toaster oven for another 5 to 7 minutes, until the cheese is slightly golden, and serve.

Ingredient Tip: Cutting the eggplant into ¼-inch slices is important for this recipe. If your slices are too thick, they'll end up crispy on the outside but raw in the middle.

WORTH THE WAIT

VEGETARIAN

VEGAN

ONE-POT

15-MINUTE

5-INGREDIENT

Greek Flatbread

Serves 1
Prep time: 10 minutes, plus 15 minutes
to marinate

The perfect mix between a salad and a sandwich, this Greek flatbread is satisfying after a long study session. If you have some of these ingredients on hand, it couldn't be easier to whip up. Throw it all together in a bowl, put it on top of a pita, and enjoy an easy, healthy, and complete meal.

½ cucumber, chopped
¼ cup kalamata olives, pitted
  and halved
¼ cup grape tomatoes, halved
2 teaspoons olive oil

1 teaspoon freshly squeezed
  lemon juice
⅛ teaspoon kosher salt
1 (6½-inch) pita bread
2 tablespoons garlic hummus

1. In a medium bowl, stir together the cucumber, olives, tomatoes, olive oil, lemon juice, and salt. Set aside for 15 minutes to marinate.

2. Place the pita on your work surface. Spread the hummus over the pita. Top with the vegetable mixture and enjoy.

Ingredient Tip: To take this to the next level, toast your pita before adding the toppings. You can also add other toppings like feta cheese, fresh dill, or a drizzle of olive oil on top.

Pesto Pasta in a Mug

Serves 1
Prep time: 5 minutes
Cook time: 15 minutes

When I was a freshman in college, I was only able to have a microwave in my room. If you crave homemade pasta, but don't have a place to boil water, this recipe is perfect for you. Adding in some fresh Parmesan cheese and black pepper will make you completely forget you ever needed a stove.

- ¾ cup dried elbow macaroni
- 2 tablespoons store-bought pesto
- 1 tablespoon grated Parmesan cheese
- Freshly ground black pepper

1. Pour the pasta into a microwave-safe mug and cover with water.

2. Microwave for 3 minutes longer than the stovetop instructions indicate on the box of pasta.

3. Drain the water out of the mug and stir in the pesto and Parmesan. Add pepper to taste.

4. Eat with a spoon directly out of the mug.

Variation Tip: While this is great with pesto, this recipe works with any store-bought sauce. Tomato, vodka, or Alfredo sauces would be perfect additions to this simple microwave pasta.

Mac and Cheese

Serves 1
Prep time: 5 minutes
Cook time: 5 minutes

Everyone might have their favorite boxed mac 'n' cheese, but I can assure you it doesn't compare to making it from scratch. By using a combination of Parmesan and cheddar to make a delectable homemade cheese sauce, this might become your new favorite.

⅓ cup dried pasta
½ cup water
¼ cup grated Parmesan cheese
½ cup shredded cheddar cheese
¼ cup 2% milk

1. In a microwave-safe bowl or large mug, combine the pasta and water. Stir with a fork and microwave for 90 seconds. Don't worry about overflow.

2. Stir again with a fork and microwave for an additional 2 minutes, until all the water has evaporated or been absorbed.

3. Stir in the Parmesan, cheddar, and milk and microwave for 1 minute. Stir with a fork before eating.

> **Cooking Tip:** Make sure your noodles are mostly cooked before adding in the cheese and milk. Some microwaves have different power levels and therefore the timing can vary.

15-Minute Lemon-Herb Salmon

Serves 1
Prep time: 5 minutes
Cook time: 10 minutes

Salmon is a go-to fish for many people because it's healthy, easy to cook, and delicious. For those who don't cook fish often, this recipe takes all the fuss out of cooking a typical fish. By seasoning it with garlic, lemon, thyme, and paprika and just throwing it in the toaster oven, this recipe makes weeknight fish an easy option.

1 tablespoon olive oil
1 garlic clove, minced
1 teaspoon freshly squeezed
   lemon juice
1 teaspoon dried thyme

1 teaspoon paprika
Kosher salt
Freshly ground black pepper
1 (4-ounce) salmon fillet

1. Preheat the toaster oven or oven to 400°F.

2. Whisk together the olive oil, garlic, lemon juice, thyme, and paprika and season with salt and pepper to taste.

3. Pat the salmon fillet dry. Line the toaster oven tray with aluminum foil and place the salmon on top.

4. Cover the salmon on both sides with the citrus-herb sauce and make sure it is spread evenly.

5. Bake for 8 to 10 minutes, or until it is cooked through and flakes easily, and serve.

Variation Tip: This recipe base is great for experimenting. You can change the flavor profile with soy sauce and sesame oil or create a blackened salmon with some chili powder and cayenne pepper. It'll allow you to enjoy a variety of different flavors while using the same basic recipe.

Juicy Turkey Meatballs

Serves 1 or 2
Prep time: 5 minutes
Cook time: 15 minutes

Served in some marinara sauce alongside some pasta or veggies, these lighter-than-beef meatballs are the ultimate comfort food.

⅓ cup bread crumbs
2 tablespoons grated Parmesan cheese
1 garlic clove, minced
¼ teaspoon dried oregano
Kosher salt

Freshly ground black pepper
1 large egg, beaten
12 ounces ground turkey
2 tablespoons olive oil
2 cups marinara sauce
1 tablespoon chopped fresh basil

1. In a mixing bowl, combine the bread crumbs, cheese, garlic, oregano, and salt and pepper to taste. Add the egg and ground turkey and mix very well. Using your hands, form 6 to 8 meatballs, each about 1¼ inches in diameter.

2. In a skillet, heat the oil over medium-high heat. Once the oil is hot, add the meatballs and cook for about 6 minutes, using tongs to turn the meatballs once, so they are browned on all sides.

3. Once the meatballs are finished cooking, add the marinara sauce to the pan and reduce the heat to a simmer. Sprinkle with basil (if using).

4. Let the meatballs simmer in the sauce for about 10 minutes. Check to make sure they are fully cooked by cutting one meatball in half to ensure it is no longer pink or using a thermometer to check that the internal temperature is 165°F.

WORTH THE WAIT

VEGETARIAN

VEGAN

ONE-POT

15-MINUTE

5-INGREDIENT

Weeknight Chicken

Serves 2
Prep time: 5 minutes
Cook time: 15 minutes

Chicken breast is a go-to protein for many but can get boring after a while. I am here to solve your chicken problems. In less than 20 minutes, using a little technique, this recipe will bring restaurant-quality chicken right to your kitchen.

2 chicken breasts
Kosher salt
Freshly ground black pepper
1 tablespoon olive oil

½ cup chicken broth
Juice of 1 lemon
2 tablespoons mustard
2 tablespoons unsalted butter

1. Season the chicken liberally on both sides with salt and pepper.

2. Heat the olive oil in a skillet over medium-high heat until hot.

3. Cook the chicken for 4 to 5 minutes per side, depending on thickness, getting a nice crust on both sides and making sure the internal temperature reaches 165°F.

4. Remove the chicken and reduce the heat to medium-low. Add the chicken broth and lemon juice, using a spatula and the liquid to scrape up the browned bits from the bottom of the pan. Cook until the liquid has reduced by half, about 5 to 7 minutes.

5. Add the mustard and butter, mixing well, and season with salt and pepper to taste.

6. Once the sauce is thickened, add the chicken back to warm it up and serve immediately.

> **Ingredient Tip:** If your chicken breasts are really thick, you can butterfly them. This means taking a sharp knife and cutting horizontally so that the pieces are half as thick. This will save you time and prevent you from undercooking the chicken.

WORTH THE WAIT

VEGETARIAN

VEGAN

ONE-POT

15-MINUTE

5-INGREDIENT

WORTH THE WAIT

VEGETARIAN

VEGAN

ONE-POT

15-MINUTE

5-INGREDIENT

Always Satisfying Cheeseburger

Serves 2
Prep time: 10 minutes
Cook time: 30 minutes

A great cheeseburger is really hard to beat. Something about the soft bun, cara-melized onions, and gooey cheese just makes me smile. This recipe is so easy, you'll forget all about your favorite burger joint.

1 tablespoon olive oil
1 tablespoon unsalted butter
1 white onion, sliced
Kosher salt
Freshly ground black pepper
1 tablespoon canola oil
1 pound ground beef, formed into 4-ounce balls
4 slices American cheese
2 to 4 hamburger buns

BURGER SAUCE

2 tablespoons mayonnaise
2 tablespoons Dijon mustard
½ teaspoon garlic powder

1. Heat the olive oil and butter in a skillet over medium-low heat, then add the onion and cook for about 20 to 30 minutes, or until slightly browned and cara-melized. Season to taste with salt and pepper. Once cooked, set aside.

2. While the onion is cooking, make the sauce by combining the mayonnaise, mustard, and garlic powder. Set aside.

3. In a separate pan over medium-high heat, warm the canola oil until smoking hot. Place the balls of ground beef in the pan for 5 seconds before putting a cup or mug on top of a metal spatula and smashing down until the patty is thin. Season with salt and pepper and cook for 2 to 3 minutes, or until crispy underneath.

4. Flip and immediately cover with a spoonful of the onion and a slice of American cheese. Cover with a lid or a larger pan so the cheese gets gooey, about 1 more minute.

5. Remove the burgers and quickly toast the buns in the pan until warm, 1 minute.

6. To assemble, put the sauce on the bottom bun, followed by your burger (or two if you're feeling yourself), followed by a little more sauce and your top bun.

Ingredient Tip: When flipping a smashed burger, be sure to really scrape underneath the patty before trying to flip. This will help you keep all the delicious crispy bits that you get from smashing the burger down in the pan.

Garlic Butter Steak

Serves 1
Prep time: 5 minutes
Cook time: 10 minutes, plus 10 minutes to rest

Whether you had a long day studying, or want to impress someone with a special meal, steak is a great choice. Garlic butter helps take this classic meal to restaurant-quality levels. Note: A rare steak will be bright red in the middle and will feel soft to the touch. A medium-rare steak will look pink with a hint of red and should give in a little when pressed. For a medium steak, the inside will have a small strip of pink but look mostly brown and should feel firm to the touch.

1 tablespoon unsalted butter, at room temperature
1 tablespoon fresh parsley, chopped
1 garlic clove, minced
1 (12-ounce) bone-in rib eye
Kosher salt
Freshly ground black pepper
1 tablespoon canola or neutral oil

1. In a small bowl, mix the butter together with the parsley and garlic. Set aside.

2. Season the steak heavily with salt and pepper on both sides. The thicker the steak, the more seasoning it will require.

3. In a skillet, heat the oil over medium-high heat. Allow the pan to get smoking hot before adding the steak.

4. Sear the steak for approximately 5 minutes on each side, or until a deep brown crust forms. Cook until the meat reaches your desired level of doneness. If you have a meat thermometer, 135°F is medium rare, 140°F to 145°F is medium, and above 150°F is well done. It is important to remember that steak will continue to cook a few more degrees once removed from the pan.

5. Remove the steak and top with the garlic butter. Let it rest for 10 minutes before serving.

Ingredient Tip: Letting your steak rest before slicing is crucial because it allows the juices to absorb back inside the meat instead of running out all over the plate. Cover your steak with aluminum foil to keep it warm while it rests.

Classic Lasagna

PAGE 98

FEASTING WITH FRIENDS

WORTH THE WAIT

VEGETARIAN

VEGAN

ONE-POT

15-MINUTE

5-INGREDIENT

Full Sunday Scramble

Serves 4
Prep time: 10 minutes
Cook time: 20 minutes

Every Sunday in college, no matter how hungover we were, my roommates and I were always determined to make a brunch that would bring us back to life. A cup of coffee, some sports on TV, and a big brunch would always do the trick. Cheesy eggs, breakfast potatoes, and homemade maple butter toast hit the spot.

5 tablespoons unsalted
  butter, divided
¼ cup maple syrup
3 tablespoons olive oil
6 medium Yukon Gold potatoes, cut
  into ½-inch cubes
1 teaspoon salt

1 teaspoon garlic powder
1 teaspoon chili powder
½ teaspoon cayenne pepper
10 large eggs
⅓ cup shredded cheddar cheese
8 slices toast

1. To make the maple butter, place 4 tablespoons of butter in a small bowl and let it soften for about 20 minutes. Once soft, add the maple syrup and mix with a fork to combine.

2. In a large sauté pan over medium heat, heat the olive oil.

3. Add the potatoes to the pan and cook for 10 to 15 minutes, stirring often, until the potatoes have a crispy exterior but are soft in the middle. Turn off the heat and add the salt, garlic powder, chili powder, and cayenne pepper. Stir to combine.

4. Crack the eggs into a separate bowl and whisk well until the mixture is homogenous.

5. In a large pan over medium-low heat, add the remaining 1 tablespoon of butter. Once the butter is fully melted, add the eggs and cook for about 6 to 8 minutes, stirring constantly with a spatula.

6. Once the eggs are still soft but no longer runny, turn off the heat, add the cheese, and season with salt and pepper to taste.

7. Serve the toast topped with maple butter alongside the eggs and potatoes.

Appliance Switch-Up: If you only have one skillet, you can easily make these potatoes in the toaster oven or oven. Just coat the potatoes in the olive oil and bake at 400°F for 30 to 40 minutes, or until crispy.

WORTH THE WAIT

VEGETARIAN

VEGAN

ONE-POT

15-MINUTE

5-INGREDIENT

Shakshuka

Serves 2 to 4
Prep time: 5 minutes
Cook time: 15 minutes

Shakshuka is an amazing Middle Eastern baked egg dish that cooks everything in one big skillet. By cooking the eggs in a savory tomato sauce, the yolks stay runny and perfect for dipping toast. This is a great, healthy brunch for a group of friends on a lazy Sunday.

3 tablespoons extra-virgin olive oil
1 onion, halved and thinly sliced
4 garlic cloves, smashed
3 bell peppers (one each red, yellow, and orange), cored and thinly sliced

1 (15-ounce) can fire-roasted diced tomatoes, drained
Sea salt
Freshly ground black pepper
4 large eggs
Chopped fresh parsley, for garnish (optional)

1. In a large skillet, heat the olive oil over medium heat. Cook the onion for 3 minutes, then add the garlic and cook for an additional 2 minutes, just until the onion has begun to soften.

2. Add the bell peppers and cook for another 5 minutes.

3. Add the tomatoes and bring to a simmer. Season with salt and pepper.

4. Make four indentations in the vegetable mixture. Carefully crack an egg into a bowl and gently pour it into one of the indentations. Repeat with the remaining eggs.

5. Cook uncovered until the whites are set and the egg yolks are still runny, about 5 minutes. Sprinkle with fresh parsley (if using).

Variation Tip: If you want to add some extra flavor to your shakshuka, go for some crumbled feta cheese or sliced avocado on top. The feta will add a salty tang, while the avocado will add some creaminess and freshness.

Three Bean Chili

Serves 5 or 6
Prep time: 10 minutes
Cook time: 15 minutes

Chili is great because all it requires is throwing a bunch of tasty ingredients into a pot, bringing them to a boil, and letting time work its magic. By using a variety of beans, you achieve a ton of flavor in a very short time. This chili is great for lunch or dinner and is easily freezable for future meals.

1 tablespoon olive oil
1 onion, chopped
4 garlic cloves, minced, or
   ½ teaspoon garlic powder
1 (28-ounce) can diced tomatoes
2 cups vegetable broth
1 (15-ounce) can kidney beans,
   drained and rinsed

1 (15-ounce) can black beans,
   drained and rinsed
1 (15-ounce) can pinto beans,
   drained and rinsed
1 (6-ounce) can tomato paste
2 tablespoons chili powder
⅛ teaspoon kosher salt

1. Heat the olive oil in a large soup pot over medium-high heat. Add the onion and garlic and sauté for about 5 minutes, or until soft.

2. Stir in the tomatoes and their juices, vegetable broth, kidney beans, black beans, pinto beans, tomato paste, chili powder, and salt. Bring to a boil and then reduce to a simmer. Cook for 10 to 15 minutes, until the chili has reduced and the flavors have come together.

3. Taste for seasoning and add more chili powder or salt as needed. Leftovers will keep in an airtight container for 1 week in the refrigerator or 1 month in the freezer.

Cooking Tip: As the chili cooks down, the flavors become more intense. For example, it may get too salty or too spicy if you add too many spices at the beginning. I recommend tasting for seasoning only toward the end of cooking.

WORTH THE WAIT   VEGETARIAN   **VEGAN**   **ONE-POT**   15-MINUTE   5-INGREDIENT

WORTH THE WAIT

VEGETARIAN

VEGAN

ONE-POT

15-MINUTE

5-INGREDIENT

Classic Lasagna

Serves 4
Prep time: 10 minutes
Cook time: 45 minutes

*Lasagna is a great college food because it's cheap and can feed a ton of people.
By using oven-ready lasagna noodles (also sometimes labeled as "no-boil"), this
recipe saves on time and cleanup while always being a true crowd-pleaser.*

1 (16-ounce) container
   ricotta cheese
½ cup grated Parmesan
   cheese, divided
1 large egg, beaten
½ teaspoon garlic powder
½ teaspoon onion powder
2 teaspoons kosher salt

1 teaspoon freshly ground
   black pepper
Nonstick cooking spray
1 cup store-bought Bolognese
   sauce, divided
1 (9-ounce) box oven-ready
   lasagna noodles
2 cups shredded low-moisture
   mozzarella cheese

1. In a bowl, mix together the ricotta, Parmesan cheese, egg, garlic powder, onion
   powder, salt, and pepper. Set aside.

2. Preheat the oven to 375°F and spray an 8-by-8-inch baking dish with cooking
   spray to prevent the lasagna from sticking.

3. Spread ⅓ cup of Bolognese sauce on the bottom of the dish. Top the sauce with
   a layer of lasagna noodles, breaking up the noodles as needed to fit them in a
   single layer.

4. Use a spatula or spoon to spread half of the ricotta mixture on top of the
   lasagna noodles, then sprinkle on one-third of the mozzarella.

5. Repeat the layers with another ⅓ cup of sauce, another layer of noodles, the remaining ricotta mixture, and half of the remaining mozzarella cheese.

6. Finish with the remaining ⅓ cup of sauce, the remaining noodles, and the rest of the mozzarella.

7. Cover the dish tightly with aluminum foil and bake for 30 minutes. Carefully remove the foil and bake for an additional 15 minutes, or until the cheese is browned and bubbly. Let cool for at least 10 minutes before serving.

Variation Tip: If you want to really impress your friends, make the Bolognese sauce yourself using the recipe on page 106. Or you can easily make this vegetarian by using marinara sauce instead.

WORTH THE WAIT

VEGETARIAN

VEGAN

ONE-POT

15-MINUTE

5-INGREDIENT

Chicken Stir-Fry

Serves 4
Prep time: 20 minutes
Cook time: 40 minutes

This recipe is perfect for when you want to feed a crowd something tasty, relatively healthy, and full of vegetables. Inspired by Chinese takeout, this dish will give you all the flavors you love while costing you a lot less money. Serve over rice noodles or any kind of rice.

FOR THE CHICKEN

2 pounds boneless, skinless chicken
   breast, cut into 1-inch cubes
1 tablespoon cornstarch
Kosher salt
Freshly ground black pepper
1 tablespoon canola oil
2 cups carrots, cut into
   ½-inch circles
3 cups broccoli, cut into
   small pieces
2 cups shiitake mushrooms, sliced
1 tablespoon soy sauce

STIR-FRY SAUCE

1 teaspoon cornstarch
½ cup chicken stock
1 tablespoon canola oil
2 tablespoons minced garlic
2 tablespoons minced ginger
1 teaspoon red pepper flakes
⅔ cup soy sauce
1 tablespoon sesame oil
2 tablespoons honey

1. Place the chicken breasts in a medium mixing bowl and add the cornstarch. Season with salt and pepper. Heat a large skillet over medium-high heat and pour in the oil to coat the bottom of the pan.

2. Cook the chicken for about 3 minutes per side, turning with tongs, cooking in batches if necessary. Set aside.

3. Add a little more oil along with the carrots and broccoli. Cook for 5 minutes, then add the mushrooms. Season with salt, pepper, and the soy sauce.

4. Cook for an additional 8 to 10 minutes, until the vegetables begin to soften and slightly brown.

5. To make the stir-fry sauce, dissolve the cornstarch in a bowl with the chicken stock.

6. In a small saucepan over medium heat, combine the canola oil, garlic, ginger, and red pepper flakes. Cook for 1 minute, then add the cornstarch mixture, soy sauce, sesame oil, and honey. Stir to combine.

7. Bring the mixture to a boil before reducing the heat to medium-low, allowing the sauce to thicken for about 5 to 7 minutes.

8. In the large skillet over medium heat, add the chicken and vegetables back to the pan, then add the sauce. Stir well to combine.

9. Cook for another 2 to 3 minutes to warm the chicken and vegetables.

10. Remove from the heat and serve.

Ingredient Tip: Cutting the chicken into 1-inch cubes is important, because it will affect the cooking time. By cutting it this small, we can cook it in minutes and make sure there aren't any raw pieces.

WORTH THE WAIT

VEGETARIAN

VEGAN

ONE-POT

15-MINUTE

5-INGREDIENT

Greek Chicken

Serves 4 to 6
Prep time: 10 minutes, plus 30 minutes to marinate
Cook time: 50 minutes

Healthy and simple, chicken breast can get overpowered in a lot of recipes. However, you will not want to have chicken any other way after trying this Greek-inspired dish, which marinates the meat in seasoned yogurt and bakes it in the oven until it gets a crispy exterior.

½ cup full-fat Greek yogurt
¼ cup olive oil
5 garlic cloves, minced
1 tablespoon oregano
1 tablespoon honey

2 tablespoons freshly squeezed lemon juice
Kosher salt
Freshly ground black pepper
3 pounds bone-in, skin-on chicken breasts

1. In a large bowl, combine the yogurt, olive oil, garlic, oregano, honey, and lemon juice and season with salt and pepper to taste. Mix well to combine.

2. Place the chicken and yogurt marinade in a large sealable plastic bag. Seal the bag and massage it to ensure that the marinade fully coats the chicken. Place the bag in the refrigerator to marinate for at least 30 minutes or up to 24 hours.

3. Remove the chicken from the refrigerator 20 minutes before cooking. Preheat the toaster oven or oven to 400°F.

4. Season both sides of the chicken heavily with salt and pepper and place on a baking sheet skin-side up.

5. Cook the chicken for 40 to 50 minutes, depending on the thickness of the chicken breast, until the outside is slightly browned and the internal temperature has reached 165°F.

Cooking Tip: Marinating any type of chicken in yogurt will help keep it flavorful and moist while cooking. The longer you let it marinate, the more flavor it will develop.

WORTH THE WAIT

VEGETARIAN

VEGAN

ONE-POT

15-MINUTE

5-INGREDIENT

Tomato-Feta Shrimp

Serves 3 or 4
Prep time: 10 minutes
Cook time: 15 minutes

One of the few recipes that has been passed down through my family, this shrimp dish is an easy staple that is one of the quickest weeknight dinners. By using frozen shrimp, spicy Greek tomato sauce, and feta, this recipe comes together quickly to create something that is greater than the sum of its parts.

1 pound frozen shrimp, defrosted and patted dry
Kosher salt
Freshly ground black pepper
1 tablespoon garlic powder
Olive oil, for greasing the pan
8 ounces store-bought tomato sauce
1 teaspoon oregano
1 teaspoon red pepper flakes
4 ounces crumbled feta cheese

1. Season the shrimp liberally on both sides with salt, pepper, and the garlic powder.

2. Preheat the toaster oven or oven to 350°F.

3. Heat a large sauté pan over medium-high heat. Coat the bottom of the pan with olive oil. Add the shrimp and sauté for about 2 minutes per side, or until slightly browned.

4. In a medium bowl, combine the tomato sauce, oregano, and red pepper flakes and mix well to combine.

5. In a large baking dish, spoon a small amount of the tomato sauce mixture to coat the bottom. Add the shrimp and cover with more sauce and the crumbled feta cheese.

6. Bake for about 10 minutes, or until the feta has just begun to melt into the sauce.

Ingredient Tip: If you have access to a freezer, frozen shrimp are a great ingredient to have on hand. They are normally high quality and cheaper than fresh shrimp.

WORTH THE WAIT

VEGETARIAN

VEGAN

ONE-POT

15-MINUTE

5-INGREDIENT

Bolognese Sauce

Serves 12
Prep time: 15 minutes
Cook time: 4 hours 45 minutes

This meal is the perfect end to any weekend. You can prep it early and then go about your day, and it's perfect for storing as leftovers to eat later in the week. Serve it with your favorite pasta. Note: If you can't find ground pork or veal, you can use 3 pounds of beef instead of 1 pound of each.

2 tablespoons olive oil
1 pound ground beef
1 pound ground pork
1 pound ground veal
Kosher salt
8 ounces bacon, cut into
  ½-inch slices
2 medium onions, diced
6 large carrots, diced

8 celery stalks, diced
8 garlic cloves, minced
1 tablespoon red pepper flakes
1 (6-ounce) tube tomato paste
2 cups red cooking wine
1 (28-ounce) can crushed tomatoes
2 cups beef broth
1 cup milk
1 tablespoon granulated sugar

1. In a large saucepan, heat the olive oil over medium-high heat. Add the ground beef, pork, and veal and cook for 6 to 10 minutes, or until the meat has begun to brown and is no longer pink. Season heavily with salt. Once cooked, transfer the meat and any remaining liquid to a bowl.

2. Next, in the same pan, cook the bacon over medium heat for 5 to 6 minutes. Add the onions, carrots, and celery and cook until the onions are translucent and soft, about 10 minutes. Add the garlic and red pepper flakes and cook for an additional 3 to 4 minutes.

3. Once the vegetables are cooked, add the tomato paste and stir to incorporate it into the vegetables. Cook down until the paste turns from a bright red to a rust color, about 4 to 6 minutes.

4. Add the cooked ground meat back to the pot, mix thoroughly, and add the red cooking wine. Cook for about 5 minutes, until the liquid has reduced by half.

5. Finally, add the tomatoes, beef broth, milk, and sugar.

6. Bring to a boil and then immediately reduce to a simmer.

7. Let simmer for about 3 to 4 hours, or until the liquid has reduced into a thick meat sauce. As always, taste for seasoning.

Prep Tip: If you have a food processor, use it to mince your vegetables. This will save you a lot of time and keep the sauce smooth instead of chunky.

Thai Peanut Noodles

Serves 2
Prep time: 5 minutes
Cook time: 5 minutes

If you're looking for a cheap and quick group meal, look no further than these noodles. Dressing up instant ramen with some peanut sauce will look impressive while also tasting great. If you are struggling to figure out what to make and have these ingredients on hand, give these noodles a shot.

> 2 packages instant ramen, seasoning packets discarded or reserved for another use
> ½ cup peanut sauce
> 2 tablespoons shredded carrots
> 1 tablespoon chopped fresh cilantro
> 2 tablespoons peanuts

1. In a saucepan on a hot plate, cook both packages of ramen together following the package instructions, doubling the amount of water.

2. Drain the noodles and transfer them to a bowl with the peanut sauce.

3. Add the carrots, cilantro, and peanuts. Toss well before serving.

Variation Tip: Add any leftovers you want to these noodles to give them some more depth. Cooked protein, vegetables, or hot sauce would all be great additions to give this dish some punch.

WORTH THE WAIT

VEGETARIAN

VEGAN

ONE-POT

15-MINUTE

5-INGREDIENT

Steak Fajitas

Serves 4
Prep time: 5 minutes
Cook time: 10 minutes, plus 5 minutes to rest

This one-pot dinner is a great recipe when you want some meat and veggies. Once you have this basic recipe down, you can easily swap in chicken, shrimp, pork, or vegetarian options. To make it a complete meal, be sure to include homemade Guacamole (page 39).

2 tablespoons canola oil, divided
1 pound skirt steak
Sea salt
Freshly ground black pepper
1 yellow onion, thinly sliced

3 bell peppers, green, red, and yellow, sliced
1 tablespoon chili powder
12 corn tortillas, warmed

1. In a large skillet, heat 1 tablespoon of oil over medium-high heat.

2. Pat the steak dry with paper towels and season both sides with salt and pepper. Add the steak to the hot skillet and sear each side for 3 to 5 minutes for medium-rare. Transfer to a cutting board to rest for 5 minutes.

3. Add the remaining 1 tablespoon of oil, onion, and bell peppers to the pan and sauté for 5 minutes, until barely tender. Season again with salt and pepper.

4. Thinly slice the beef and return it to the pan, along with any accumulated juices. Add the chili powder. Cook for about 1 minute, until the spices are distributed. Taste for seasoning one more time.

5. Serve with the warmed corn tortillas.

Ingredient Tip: There are two ways I like to warm my corn tortillas. If you are working with an actual gas flame, char the tortillas directly over the flame on medium-low heat for 30 seconds per side. If you have a hot plate, heat the tortillas in a skillet over medium heat for 30 seconds per side.

Berry Crumble
PAGE 113

Chapter 8

DESSERTS

Raspberry-Mint Sorbet

Serves 6
Prep time: 5 minutes, plus 4 hours
to freeze

This is one of the easiest and most refreshing desserts to serve during the warm summer months. By throwing raspberries in a blender with some simple add-ins, you can impress your friends with a post-dinner treat worthy of a five-star restaurant.

2 cups frozen raspberries
½ cup fresh mint
¼ cup honey
1 tablespoon vanilla
1 to 2 cups ice

1. In a blender, combine the frozen raspberries, mint, honey, vanilla, and ice. You may need to add water until the mixture has the consistency of a slushie.

2. Put the mixture in a freezer-safe container and place in the freezer to chill for at least 4 hours to let the sorbet set up.

3. Remove from the freezer 20 minutes before serving to allow the sorbet to slightly defrost.

Ingredient Tip: Fresh raspberries will add an amazing freshness that frozen raspberries just can't offer. Just note that you will need more ice if you're not using frozen berries.

Berry Crumble

Serves 1
Prep time: 5 minutes
Cook time: 5 minutes

A berry crumble has the perfect combination of tartness from the fruit combined with the comfort of a sweet, buttery crust. By downsizing a traditional crumble recipe to fit a microwave, you can enjoy this amazing berry crumble in less than 5 minutes.

1 tablespoon unsalted butter
¼ cup quick-cooking oats
¾ cup frozen berries, thawed
1 teaspoon granulated sugar
½ teaspoon cornstarch
½ tablespoon powdered sugar (optional)

1. In a small microwave-safe bowl, microwave the butter for 25 seconds, or until melted. Add the oats and mix until they are completely coated in the butter.

2. In a large, microwave-safe mug, mix together the berries, sugar, and cornstarch. Scoop the oats on top of the berry mixture and spread them out evenly.

3. Microwave on high for 90 seconds, or until the berries are bubbling. If the berries are not bubbling yet, microwave for another 30 seconds.

4. Let cool for 2 minutes and dust with powdered sugar (if using) before eating.

Variation Tip: If you prefer a crisper texture, throw this in the toaster oven for a minute before serving. I always like to top my berry crumble with some vanilla ice cream. The cold ice cream and warm berries complement each other perfectly.

WORTH THE WAIT

VEGETARIAN

VEGAN

ONE-POT

15-MINUTE

5-INGREDIENT

WORTH THE WAIT

VEGETARIAN

VEGAN

ONE-POT

15-MINUTE

5-INGREDIENT

Apple Crisp for One

Serves 1
Prep time: 10 minutes
Cook time: 5 minutes

Apple pie is an American classic that most people love to eat but sometimes hate to make. By replacing the crust with some simple, hassle-free ingredients, you can enjoy this delicious flavor combination without all the fuss. Just don't skimp on the vanilla ice cream.

2 teaspoons all-purpose flour, divided

2½ teaspoons granulated sugar, divided

⅜ teaspoon ground cinnamon, divided

1 tablespoon cold unsalted butter, diced

1 Granny Smith apple, peeled, cored, and diced

½ teaspoon freshly squeezed lemon juice

Ice cream, for serving (optional)

1. In a small bowl, stir together 1 teaspoon of flour, 1½ of teaspoons sugar, and ⅛ teaspoon of cinnamon.

2. Add the butter and mix it in using a fork, breaking up the mixture to form small crumbles and make a streusel. Set aside.

3. In a microwave-safe mug, stir together the apple, remaining 1 teaspoon of flour, remaining 1 teaspoon of sugar, lemon juice, and the remaining ¼ teaspoon of cinnamon.

4. Sprinkle the streusel in an even layer over the top of the apple mixture.

5. Microwave the crisp for 2 to 2½ minutes, or until the apples are tender. Serve with a scoop of ice cream (if using).

"Grilled" Pineapple

Serves 6
Prep time: 10 minutes
Cook time: 10 minutes

If you've ever been to a Brazilian steakhouse, or churrascaria, you know about the huge salad bar and the 20 types of unlimited meats on offer. But what I truly love about that meal, over anything else, is the sweet and spicy grilled pineapple. Cut into slices, served warm, and soul-warming, it is one of my favorite desserts of all time. Here's how to make it without doing any actual grilling.

½ cup maple syrup
½ cup brown sugar
1 teaspoon kosher salt
1 teaspoon cayenne pepper
1 pineapple, cut into 1-inch-thick slices
4 tablespoons butter

1. In a small bowl, combine the maple syrup, brown sugar, salt, and cayenne pepper. Mix well.

2. Liberally brush both sides of all pineapple slices in the marinade and set aside.

3. In a medium skillet over medium heat, melt the butter.

4. Add the pineapple and cook for 4 minutes per side, just until the sugar is caramelized but not burnt.

Ingredient Tip: If you don't want to go through the hassle of cutting a whole pineapple, many grocery stores carry cubed fresh pineapple. While you'll have to adjust the glaze and cook time, this is a better option for making a smaller batch of this dessert.

WORTH THE WAIT

VEGETARIAN

VEGAN

ONE-POT

15-MINUTE

5-INGREDIENT

WORTH THE WAIT

VEGETARIAN

VEGAN

ONE-POT

15-MINUTE

5-INGREDIENT

Vegan Chocolate Pudding

Serves 1
Prep time: 5 minutes

Something about a chocolate pudding cup just brings me back to the best parts of my childhood. Using a banana and an avocado to replace the typical pudding base, this recipe is vegan and makes a classic dessert much healthier.

1 banana
2 to 4 tablespoons soy milk
2 tablespoons unsweetened cocoa powder
2 tablespoons granulated sugar
½ ripe avocado

1. In a blender, combine the banana, soy milk, cocoa powder, sugar, and avocado. Puree until smooth.

2. If you're using a larger blender, you may need to add more milk to get the mixture completely smooth.

3. Chill in the refrigerator until the pudding has set.

Variation Tip: To make this pudding slightly more decadent, add some dark chocolate chips, fresh berries, or even caramel sauce.

Snickerdoodle Skillet Cookie

Serves 8
Prep time: 5 minutes
Cook time: 30 minutes

Snickerdoodle cookies combine the flavors of cinnamon and sugar for an addictive, comforting dessert. This skillet version is perfect to share among a big group of friends.

Nonstick cooking spray, for greasing the pan
½ cup (packed) brown sugar
½ cup granulated sugar, plus more for topping
¼ cup (½ stick) salted butter, melted

1 tablespoon ground cinnamon, plus more for topping
1 large egg
1 teaspoon vanilla extract
1 cup all-purpose flour
¼ teaspoon baking soda

1. Preheat the oven to 375°F. Grease a 10-inch oven-safe (cast-iron or stainless steel) skillet with the cooking spray.

2. In a large bowl, stir together the brown sugar, granulated sugar, butter, and cinnamon until there aren't any large lumps.

3. Add the egg and vanilla, stirring to combine.

4. Add the flour and baking soda and stir until a thick dough forms. Use your hands to mix at the end, if needed.

5. Press the dough firmly into the skillet and sprinkle with additional granulated sugar and cinnamon.

6. Bake the cookie for 20 minutes, or until the edges are golden and the center is baked through.

7. Allow the cookie to cool, then serve it in the skillet or turn the skillet over to release it and slice it into 8 wedges.

WORTH THE WAIT

VEGETARIAN

VEGAN

ONE-POT

15-MINUTE

5-INGREDIENT

WORTH THE WAIT

VEGETARIAN

VEGAN

ONE-POT

15-MINUTE

5-INGREDIENT

Toaster Oven S'mores

Serves 2
Prep time: 5 minutes
Cook time: 1 minute

These s'mores give you the amazing memories of sitting by a campfire roasting marshmallows without ever having to set up a tent or swat away bugs. By using three ingredients that can easily be kept in your pantry, this dessert is perfect for treating yourself after a long day of studying or acing a test.

2 graham crackers, broken in half
1 chocolate bar, broken in half
2 jumbo marshmallows

1. Place the graham cracker halves on the toaster oven tray. Top each with a piece of chocolate.

2. Turn the marshmallows on their sides and place them on the chocolate, so the marshmallows appear short and wide, not tall.

3. If your toaster oven has a top rack you can remove, do so. Set the toaster oven or oven to broil. Bake the s'mores for 30 to 45 seconds, until the marshmallows are puffy and lightly golden.

4. Remove them from the toaster oven and top with the remaining 2 graham cracker halves to form sandwiches.

Cooking Tip: The broil function on a toaster oven is great because it allows items to melt and char really quickly. However, because the heat is so high, try not to take your eye off them as they can go from golden and toasted to burnt in a short amount of time.

Chocolate–Peanut Butter Cups

Serves 4
Prep time: 10 minutes, plus 1 hour to chill

Decadent but healthier than the store-bought version, these guilt-free chocolate–peanut butter cups are simply amazing. The classic flavor of peanut butter and chocolate is still there, but these will keep you both energized and full. This is one of the best replacements for any candy or snack you can get at your local store.

1½ cups chopped pitted dates
1 cup walnut halves and pieces
¼ cup peanut butter
2 tablespoons unsweetened cocoa powder
2 teaspoons vanilla extract

1. Place the dates, walnuts, peanut butter, cocoa powder, and vanilla in a food processor and pulse until a sticky dough forms. It should stick together when pressed between your fingers. If the mixture is too loose, add some more dates and walnuts.

2. Line a loaf pan with parchment paper and press the dough into the pan evenly.

3. Chill the mixture in the refrigerator for at least 1 hour.

4. Remove the chilled dough from the pan by lifting it out using the parchment paper. Transfer to a cutting board and cut into 4 bars.

Ingredient Tip: If you want classic chocolate–peanut butter cups, skip the dates and add more nuts until a firm dough forms. While the dates add a nice fruity flavor, some people prefer the traditional version.

WORTH THE WAIT

VEGETARIAN

VEGAN

ONE-POT

15-MINUTE

5-INGREDIENT

Microwave Brownie

Serves 1
Prep time: 5 minutes
Cook time: 2 minutes

Have you ever craved a brownie, but didn't want the temptation of an entire tray? This recipe is a genius hack, as you can have a single brownie without the temptation or feeling guilty that you ate too many. If you're treating yourself and decide you want another, this recipe comes together in about 5 minutes.

¼ cup granulated sugar

3 tablespoons cocoa powder

2 tablespoons canola or vegetable oil

¼ cup water

2 tablespoons brown sugar

Pinch kosher salt

¼ cup all-purpose flour

3 tablespoons chocolate chips

Splash vanilla extract

1. In a large microwave-safe mug, whisk together the granulated sugar, cocoa powder, oil, water, brown sugar, and salt.

2. Stir in the flour, chocolate chips, and vanilla extract.

3. Microwave on high for 80 seconds.

4. Remove from the microwave and let cool for 2 minutes before eating.

Ingredient Tip: Switch things up with milk chocolate, semisweet chocolate, or dark chocolate chips, or try totally different flavors like white chocolate or peanut butter chips.

Chocolate Chip Cookie in a Mug

Serves 1
Prep time: 5 minutes
Cook time: 1 minute

Everyone loves chocolate chip cookies. The problem, however, is that you usually make a huge batch with way too many left over. By changing the recipe to be made in a single-serving mug, you can satisfy that craving without dessert overload. And it's much less messy, too.

1 tablespoon unsalted butter
1 tablespoon granulated sugar
½ tablespoon light brown sugar
Pinch kosher salt

¼ teaspoon vanilla extract
1 large egg yolk
3 tablespoons all-purpose flour
2 tablespoons chocolate chips

1. In a large mug, microwave the butter for 15 seconds.

2. Add the granulated sugar, light brown sugar, salt, vanilla, and egg yolk. Mix well.

3. Add the all-purpose flour and stir well.

4. Add the chocolate chips and stir well.

5. Microwave for 45 seconds.

Ingredient Tip: If you have never separated an egg yolk from an egg white, no need to worry. Simply crack an egg into a small bowl and carefully pick up the yolk in one clean hand. Carefully transfer it from hand to hand, holding it with slightly outspread fingers, until the yolk is completely separated from the white, then place it in a separate bowl.

WORTH THE WAIT

VEGETARIAN

VEGAN

ONE-POT

15-MINUTE

5-INGREDIENT

Measurement Conversions

Volume Equivalents	U.S. Standard	U.S. Standard (ounces)	Metric (approximate)
Liquid	2 tablespoons	1 fl. oz.	30 mL
	¼ cup	2 fl. oz.	60 mL
	½ cup	4 fl. oz.	120 mL
	1 cup	8 fl. oz.	240 mL
	1½ cups	12 fl. oz.	355 mL
	2 cups or 1 pint	16 fl. oz.	475 mL
	4 cups or 1 quart	32 fl. oz.	1 L
	1 gallon	128 fl. oz.	4 L
Dry	⅛ teaspoon	–	0.5 mL
	¼ teaspoon	–	1 mL
	½ teaspoon	–	2 mL
	¾ teaspoon	–	4 mL
	1 teaspoon	–	5 mL
	1 tablespoon	–	15 mL
	¼ cup	–	59 mL
	⅓ cup	–	79 mL
	½ cup	–	118 mL
	⅔ cup	–	156 mL
	¾ cup	–	177 mL
	1 cup	–	235 mL
	2 cups or 1 pint	–	475 mL
	3 cups	–	700 mL
	4 cups or 1 quart	–	1 L
	½ gallon	–	2 L
	1 gallon	–	4 L

Oven Temperatures

Fahrenheit	Celsius (approximate)
250°F	120°C
300°F	150°C
325°F	165°C
350°F	180°C
375°F	190°C
400°F	200°C
425°F	220°C
450°F	230°C

Weight Equivalents

U.S. Standard	Metric (approximate)
½ ounce	15 g
1 ounce	30 g
2 ounces	60 g
4 ounces	115 g
8 ounces	225 g
12 ounces	340 g
16 ounces or 1 pound	455 g

Index

ACKNOWLEDGMENTS

I want to thank the countless people who have led me to this point in my life. My parents and siblings have encouraged me, supported me, and trusted me through this entire process. My late grandparents helped me truly understand that life is too short to not prioritize doing what you love. To my close friends: Your unwavering support has been a mainstay throughout my entire life; our friendship is one of a kind. Finally, to Rockridge Press, for believing in my ability and giving me the opportunity to express my culinary voice. I am forever grateful.

ABOUT THE AUTHOR

 **Noah Daniel Stern** is a self-taught home cook from New York City. He has been cooking since he was diagnosed with celiac disease in 2011, when he was disappointed with the safe food options at his disposal. Since then, his passion for cooking has led him to develop countless recipes, cook at dinner parties for hire, and advocate for young adults to improve their kitchen skills. After graduating from University of Wisconsin in 2015, he moved back to New York to pursue a career in the restaurant industry. Currently a student at the Institute of Culinary Education, he hopes to work in restaurant management and eventually own and operate his own food business.